AN INTRODUCTION TO BIBLE TRUTHS

A WORKBOOK

Thomas Albert Weaver II & Emily Weaver

authorHOUSE

AuthorHouse™
1663 Liberty Drive
Bloomington, IN 47403
www.authorhouse.com
Phone: 833-262-8899

Published by AuthorHouse 03/20/2023

ISBN: 978-1-6655-5700-9 (sc)
ISBN: 978-1-6655-5699-6 (e)

FOREWORD

Who made you? God
What else did God make? God made all things

These are the first two questions in the *Catechism for Young Children*, published by John Knox Press in 1840. It is a compilation of basic Biblical Doctrine made available and understandable. My sister, Mary Ella, and I grew up with these truths being taught to us in our home and in our church. Forty-eight years later, the Holy Spirit continues to use this framework of definitions and concepts to guide us for His glory and our greater good. We pray that God will continue His work for good in your family!

This workbook has separate lessons on each page. They contain our father's art and simple parts of our family's early history told through a little girl named MEW and a little boy named IV as they are enjoying each other and their friends. Their conversations and activities are being used to illustrate basic truths.

When our father began to write this, he would often show us the pictures. We thought Dad had always been an entertaining artist with his funny little people. We were accustomed to seeing his work. Little did we know that many years later with our own families, these lessons and illustrations would continue to be shared, even in this publication.

We invite you to go through this study with your children and answer the questions for yourself. Enjoy God's presence as He speaks to your family, or if you are a teacher, as He speaks to your class.

Precepts are the concepts of scripture that remain absolute for all time. This workbook is full of them! Every question/answer can be supported with Bible chapter and verse! Thank you for taking this opportunity to study.

From our families to yours, may King Jesus bless you throughout these pages!

Pastor Thomas Weaver, III
Mary Ella Weaver Ross
December 2021

A Workbook

An Introduction to Bible Truths

by

Thomas A. Weaver, II
Emily Hyatt Weaver

A Workbook, An Introduction to Bible Truths, is a systematic study in the Word of God, using the *Catechism for Young Children*, printed by the John Knox Press, 1840, as the point of departure. Each workbook page is complete and geared for young minds, preferably elementary. The purpose of this study is to introduce the child to the great doctrines of the Bible, to teach him/her the principles of the inductive method of Bible study, and to set the child on the road of obedience to the Word of God.

Catechism for Young Children

Question 1

Who made you?
God.

Hi, student!
This is a brand-new year.
I want to be your brand-new friend!
My name is IV, which is my nickname.
In a few more weeks, I will tell you why it is my nickname.
I have a sister who is one year younger than I.
Her name is Kitty, which is her nickname.
Her initials spell "M.E.W." Now you know why we call her Kitty?

WHAT IS YOUR NAME?

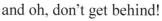

DO YOU HAVE A NICKNAME?

_____

We have just met each other, but I know something about you!
And you know something about me and about Kitty!
Do you know what it is?
It is this: God made you, God made me, and God made Kitty!
Isn't that grand?
You and I have been made by God! We are very special.
In this study this year, we are going to find out how special we are and also have a lot of fun!
Just be sure to do your homework,
and oh, don't get behind!

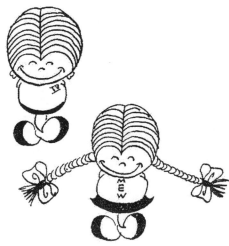

Question 2

What else did God make?
God made all things.

Hi, student!

Have you memorized the answer to Catechism Question 1?

WHO MADE YOU? _____

But God made much more than just you, me, and Kitty.

WHAT ELSE DID GOD MAKE? GOD MADE _____ THINGS.

This past summer my family stayed at a place called **Rivermont**.

It is a beautiful group of old mountain cabins on a wide river.

There was a fishpond next to a garden with flowers, vegetables, and beehives.

There were pathways and driveways.

Now Rivermont did not "just happen."

It was planned by a Christian family who loves God.

They wanted to make Rivermont beautiful, just like God made His world beautiful.

God planned a world full of trees and flowers and animals.

Then God made everything just as He had planned it.

No part of our beautiful world is here by accident. Everything has been made by God.

Question 3

> **Why did God make you and all things?**
> For His own glory.

One time a lady spoke at our Church.
Her name was Mama Kellensberger.
She was a missionary who had gone to Africa.
She said that whenever she was in the mountains,
all she could think of was one word. That word was "Glory"!
She said that God had made the mountains so beautiful and grand that the word, **glory**, was
the only word that described them.

When God made you, He had something beautiful and grand in mind.
He did not make you as a rock.
He did not make you as a puppy dog.
He did not make you as an oak tree.
HE MADE YOU A _____. (BOY or GIRL)
But, more importantly,
He made you for His own glory.
Whenever you look in the mirror at yourself,
you see something wonderful about God.
Whenever you look at what God has created around you,
you see something wonderful about God.
The Bible tells us from Isaiah 6:3 that "…the whole earth is full of His glory."

Question 4

> **How can you glorify God?**
> By loving Him and doing what He commands.

God made you and me. God made us for His own glory.

God made us to love Him and to obey Him.

One day when the Lord Jesus lived here on earth, He was teaching and said,

"A new command I give you:

Love one another as I have loved you …

You are my friend if you love one another." John 13:34-45

If you really love someone, you will want to do special things for that person.

TALK ABOUT IT:

How can you show love to these people each day?

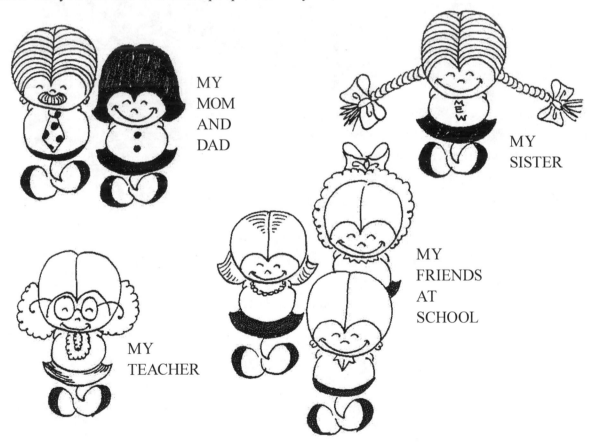

MY
MOM
AND
DAD

MY
SISTER

MY
TEACHER

MY
FRIENDS
AT
SCHOOL

Question 5

> ### Why ought you to glorify God?
> Because He made me and takes care of me.

A long, long time ago, there was a terrible battle.
It was a battle between two armies: Israel and Babylon.
Babylon was much stronger than Israel, so Babylon won the battle.
It was a sad, sad time for the nation of Israel.
There was a man who lived in Israel at that time named Jeremiah.
Jeremiah loved God with all his heart.
Even though the battle was horrible, and many people were killed,
Jeremiah knew that God was still with Israel.
After the battle, Jeremiah was able to thank God for His love.
He said to God, "Great is Your faithfulness."
Student, every day many things happen to us.
Sometimes there are good things that happen to us,
like a good grade on our Spelling test.
Sometimes there are bad things that happen to us,
like falling off our bicycle.
But no matter what happens to us, God is taking care of us.
And He takes care of us because He loves us.

TALK ABOUT IT:
Can you think of a special way
in which God has cared for you this week?
Do you know someone who needs God's special care at this time?
What can you do to help them?

Catechism for Young Children

Check-up for **Questions 1-5**

LET'S SEE IF YOU CAN MATCH THE QUESTION ON THE LEFT WITH THE ANSWER ON THE RIGHT!

****

1. Who made you?   By loving Him and doing what
                                                           He commands.

2. What else did God make?   For His own glory.

3. Why did God make you and all things?   God.

4. How can you glorify God?   Because He made me and
                                                          takes care of me.

5. Why should you glorify God?   God made all things.

Question 6

> **Are there more Gods than one**?
> There is only one God.

Student,
I was so surprised while I was studying for our lesson today.
I found out that many, many, many people in our world worship false gods.
I thought people only did that in Bible times! How wrong I was!
There is a very exciting story in the Bible about a man– just one man– who loved the Lord God with all his heart.
One day he stood up against 850 men who worshipped false gods.
Your teacher will read this exciting story.
It is found in I KINGS 18:16-39.

WHO WAS THE MAN WHO LOVED THE LORD GOD WITH ALL HIS HEART?

_____

WHO ARE THE FALSE GODS OF THIS STORY?

_____

But there are also other false gods that people worship in our country today.
Can you write out the names of these false gods?

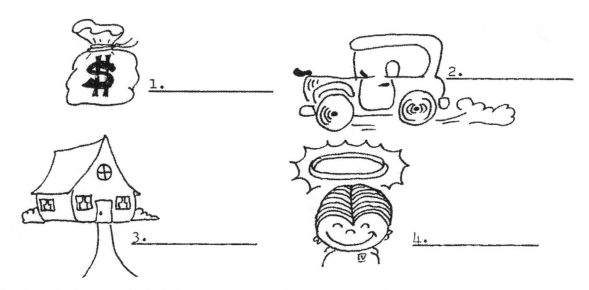

Student, isn't it wonderful that we can worship the Lord God?
Better make sure that YOU are not worshipping anything else!

Question 7

> **In how many persons does this one God exist**?
> In three persons.

I HOPE THAT YOU ARE LEARNING TO ADD IN SCHOOL.
LET'S TRY SOME ADDITION.

If I had one 🍎 and someone gave me another, 🍎

how many would I have? _____

Now if I have two, 🍎 🍎 and someone gave me another, 🍎 how many would I

then have? _____

One 🍎 plus one 🍎 plus one 🍎 makes _____. Yes, you are really good

at this addition!

Now here is a problem: There is only one true God, but He exists in three persons. This means, He is three persons. This is very hard for us to understand.

One God = Three persons!
Maybe we can understand it a little bit by looking at a three-leaf clover.

There is one clover but three leaves! One = Three
This is a little bit like God.
He is **one God**, but He is **three persons**.

CAN YOU THINK OF ANYTHING ELSE THAT ILLUSTRATES GOD? _____
In our next lesson we will find out the names of the three persons of God. We say, "the Godhead."

CAN YOU NUMBER THE LEAVES OF THE CLOVER?
WOULD YOU LIKE TO COLOR THE APPLES ON THIS PAGE?
Remember, apples come in at least three colors -- red, yellow, and green … Make them colorful!

Question 8

> **What are they**?
> The Father, the Son, and the Holy Ghost.

Today I want to introduce you to some very important people in my life. They are

My father

My grandfather,

and My great-grandfather!!

All of our names are exactly the same, except for the number after the names. The numbers are Roman numerals. Your teacher will explain what Roman Numerals are!

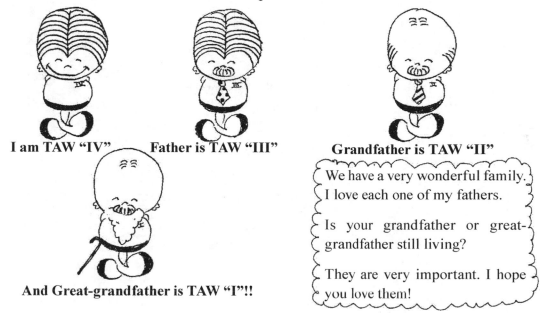

I am TAW "IV"   **Father is TAW "III"**   **Grandfather is TAW "II"**

And Great-grandfather is TAW "I"!!

> We have a very wonderful family. I love each one of my fathers.
>
> Is your grandfather or great-grandfather still living?
>
> They are very important. I hope you love them!

My three fathers are three different persons: Father, Grandfather, and Great-grandfather. But they all have the same name:

God is just a little bit like that. He is three persons, but one God. He is **not** three Gods. He is **only** one God. But He is three persons.

WHO ARE THE THREE PERSONS OF THE ONE GOD, ACCORDING TO QUESTION 8?

1. _____
2. _____
3. _____

Question 9

> **What is God?**
> God is a Spirit and has not a body like men.

My dad and I went on a hiking trip last summer!
We hiked for five days on the Appalachian Trail in North Carolina.
There were four other dads and four other sons with us.
Every day we hiked as far as we could.
And every night, we camped out!

At night, it was very, very dark.
There were no streetlights in the woods.
But we had a big campfire each night.

After our supper, we would ask our dads to tell us ghost stories.
Ghost stories are extra scary around a campfire!

Sometimes when we think about God
we think about Him as a Ghost!
I guess we think about Him as a Ghost
because He is a Spirit and does not have a body.
But God is not a ghost.
He is a Person. He is a Spirit.
That means that we cannot see Him.
But God is still very **real** because He can **think**, and **talk**, and **see**, and **move**, and **love**!

DOES GOD HAVE A BODY? _____

WHY DOES GOD <u>NOT</u> HAVE A BODY? _____

_____

DISCUSS IN CLASS:
Even though God does not have a body, how does He show that He is a **person**?

Question 10

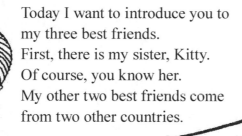

> **Where is God**?
> God is everywhere.

Today I want to introduce you to
my three best friends.
First, there is my sister, Kitty.
Of course, you know her.
My other two best friends come
from two other countries.

There is my friend, Heidi. He is from Japan.
There is my friend, Bassy. He is from Jamaica.
Both of them live on islands. Jamaica is very warm all year,
so Bassy goes bare foot a lot!

I wanted you to meet these friends so that I can help
you understand the question for today.

Kitty and I are from America. We cannot be in
Japan or Jamaica unless we go there. But if we go to
Japan or Jamaica, we will not be in our country, America.
We can only be in **one place at a time**!

But God is everywhere at once!
He is here in America. He is also in
Japan and Jamaica, at the same time!

He is with you, and He is also with everyone else
in the world!

He is here in our world, on our planet, and He is
with every star in the universe!

God is everywhere because He is a Spirit and does
not have a body like men.

GOD IS _____!

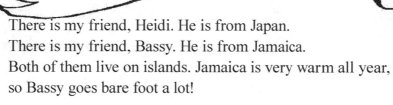

Question 11

> **<u>Can you see God</u>?**
> No, I cannot see God, but He always sees me.

One of my favorite games is Hide and Seek.
It is especially fun when played in the dark.
It's also scary!
The finder never knows when someone is going to say, "BOO!"

Even though we might hide from each other,
we can never hide from God.

No matter where I am,
God is there.

Because He is everywhere,
He always sees me.

WHY CAN WE NOT SEE GOD? _____

_____

Just before Jesus went back to heaven, He gave us a **command** and then He gave us a **promise**.

The **command** and the **promise** are found within the verses of Matthew 28:18-20;

> **"All authority in heaven and on earth has been given to me.**
> **Therefore, go and make disciples of all nations… and surely**
> **I will be with you always…"**

Do you see the promise? Fill in the missing word:
"I WILL BE WITH YOU _____."

Question 12

> **Does God know all things**?
> Yes, nothing can be hid from God.

Hi, Student!

This morning in my Quiet Time I was reading a from the Gospel of Luke … actually, Luke 15. Do you know what a Quiet Time is? It is a very special time we may have each day, alone with our heavenly Father. He talks to us through His Word, and we talk with Him through prayer. If you do not have a daily Quiet Time, this is a good time to get started!
In Luke 15, Jesus talks about three things that were lost.

AS YOU READ THIS CHAPTER (LUKE 15:1-24) MATCH UP THE THINGS THAT WERE LOST WITH THE ONE WHO FOUND THEM.

Student, the important thing to remember about this lesson is that even though **you** might lose things and not know where they are, **nothing can be hidden from God**.

We cannot hide from God. We cannot hide our thoughts from God.
He knows all about us. He knows what is in our hearts. He knows what we are thinking.
It is important each day to make sure that all of our thoughts, all of our words, and all of our actions are pleasing to our heavenly Father!

Question 13

> **<u>Can God do all things</u>?**
> Yes, God can do all His holy will.

Student, today I want to teach you some new words, some **big** words!
Maybe you have seen the Walt Disney movie, *Mary Poppins.*
Well, Mary Poppins taught a little girl and boy a very big word.
Do you remember what the word was? Right!

SUPERCALIFRAGILISTICEXPIALIDOUSIOUS! **Wow!!!**

Today I have some **big** words for you!
You can try them out on your mom and dad!

The first word is **omnipresent.** The first four letters in the word mean "all." Omnipresent means "all present." This word is only used for God. It means that He is everywhere at the same time. Remember, we talked about that in Question 10.

The second word is **omnipotent**! "Potent" means powerful.
So if you put **omni** (all) and **potent** (powerful) together, what do you have?
Right! "**All Powerful**!" This word also is used only for God.
It means that God can do **anything!**

But there is a catch to it. God can do anything in line with His holy will.

There are some things that God **cannot do** because He is **holy**.
Your teacher will read two Scriptures and you write in the blanks what God cannot do.

HEBREWS 6:18 _____

JAMES 1:13_____

CIRCLE THE NUMBER BELOW THAT IS
NOT TRUE ABOUT GOD:

1. God can do all His holy will.
2. God can be everywhere at the same time.
3. God can lie.
4. God is Omnipotent.

Question 14

> <u>**Where do you learn how to love and obey God**</u>?
> In the Bible alone

Did I ever pull a Boo-boo!

My mom asked me to paint the kitchen last week. She said that the paint would be in the storage room. When I had time to paint the kitchen, she was not at home, and I picked up the wrong can of paint! Because I did not follow all her instructions, I painted the whole kitchen with the wrong stuff, actually the glue for the floor tile! After she ordered wall paneling from the Building Supply Store and put it up, I had to do the whole kitchen all over again. All because I did not follow the instructions! I hope I never do that again. My mom does, too!

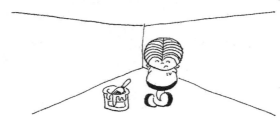

I began to think that God's Word is like a set of instructions. The Bible teaches how to love and obey God. If we don't read it, then we won't know how to really love and obey God.

Wouldn't it be terrible if we were not loving Him like we should be loving Him, or if we were not obeying Him with correct behavior? It's important to read and know God's Word!

Your teacher will read you two verses from God's Word. What do these two verses say His Word is like?

I PETER 2:2   M _____

I CORINTHIANS 3:2   M _____

WHO DRINKS **MILK** ALL THE TIME? A BABY OR A MAN? _____

WHO CAN EAT **MEAT** AND DRINK **MILK**? A BABY OR A MAN? _____

The more we read, love, and obey God's Word, the more we will understand it.
God wants us to love His Word and obey it.
He wants us to grow so that we will not be "Spiritual babies" all our lives! He wants us to grow to be "Strong men and women."

Question 15

> ### <u>Who wrote the Bible</u>?
> Holy men who were taught by the Holy Ghost.

Hi, student! I go to a school where one of our subjects is Bible. Along with spelling, writing, reading, history, and math, we have Bible. And it's not easy! Today we had a test in Bible. We were to write down who wrote the following books in the Bible:

Genesis   **Thessalonians**

Ecclesiastes   **Revelation**!

Lamentations

I had trouble just saying the names of the books! Do you know who wrote these books?

I have learned in Bible this year that there are 66 books in the Bible. The Bible is a **Library of Books bound into one book**! God used many men to write the books in the Bible.

Moses was the first man God used to write some of the books of the Bible. Moses wrote the first <u>five</u> books of the Bible. Can you say the names of these five books?

The **Apostle John** was the last man God used to write the last book in the Bible. Do you know the name of that very last book?

Each man God used was very special. His heart belonged completely to God. His actions showed love for God, and he tried every day to obey God's instructions. Each man is now in heaven.

WHAT KIND OF MEN DID GOD USE TO WRITE THE BIBLE? _____

WHO CAUSED THESE MEN TO WRITE JUST THE RIGHT WORDS? _____

God used all kinds of men to write the Bible!

Question 16

> **<u>Who were our first parents</u>?**
> Adam and Eve.

Today, I need you to think really hard!

WHAT IS YOUR MOTHER'S NAME? _____

WHAT IS YOUR FATHER'S NAME? _____

WHAT IS ONE OF YOUR GRANDPARENTS' NAME? _____

Now, keep thinking!
I want you to go as far back as you can think and tell me our **first parents'** names.

That means you will go back hundreds and hundreds of years, and thousands and thousands of years to the very first people God created on this earth.
They were our **first parents!**

PUT THEIR NAMES IN THE BLANKS BELOW.

MAN_____ _____WOMAN

Just think – **All of us** came from these two people!
That makes **all of us** kind of like cousins, doesn't it! Wow!

Adam and Eve were two very real people. They were not people of fairy tales. They were created by God, and they were very important to Him.

TURN TO GENESIS 1:31.
Fill in these blanks.

GENESIS 1:31 "GOD SAW _____ THAT HE HAD MADE,

AND IT WAS V_____   G_____."

After God created the whole world and everything in it, and after He created **Adam and Eve**, He was very pleased with what He had done.

Question 17

Of what were our first parents made?
God made the body of Adam out of the ground and formed Eve from the body of Adam.

Hi, student! Today we were given a science project in my class. We were to make **Clay-Dough!** Do you know how to make Clay-Dough? It is very easy!

These are the **ingredients**:   4 cups of flour
2 cups of salt
4 cups of water
4 tablespoons of oil
2 tablespoons cream of tarter
2-3 drops of oil
Food Coloring

This is **how** you make it: _____

Mix all ingredients in a large pan. Cook over medium heat, stirring often, until mixture is no longer sticky. The dough will be very thick. Add the food coloring. Knead the dough until it is smooth. Knead means mash and fold it. Store it in an air-tight container.

I hope you will be able to make a batch of Clay-Dough. For our science project, we are to make a Man and a Woman just like Adam and Eve.

Do you remember how God made Adam and Eve? Maybe you can look up how they were made in GENESIS 2:7-22, 26-31. After reading, answer these questions:

WHOM DID GOD MAKE FIRST?   ADAM   EVE   (circle one)

WHAT DID GOD USE TO MAKE THE MAN? _____

WHAT DID GOD USE TO MAKE THE WOMAN? _____

WHERE DID GOD PUT THE MAN AND WOMAN? _____

The man and woman I made for my science project turned out really well. They looked like Gingerbread men!

I'll bet that Adam and Eve didn't look like Gingerbread men!

Question 18

> **What did God give Adam and Eve besides bodies**?
> He gave them souls that could never die.

This has been the saddest week of my life!

My granddaddy has been sick for a long, long time. Do you remember me introducing Dad and Grandfather and Great-grandfather to you? I did that in Question 8.
My great-grandfather died long before I was born, and I never knew him. But Grandfather has always been close to me. We called him Granddaddy. Each summer, Granddaddy and Grandmother would invite Kitty and me to spend a week with them. They were always so much fun. They didn't scold us nearly as much as Mom and Dad!

A few weeks ago Granddaddy became very sick and had to go to the hospital. Four days ago he died. Kitty and I were so sad! Today we went to his funeral.

The minister told us that Granddaddy was a Christian. I knew that because Granddaddy talked often about Jesus. He prayed with me and helped me to memorize Bible verses.

At the funeral, the minister reminded us of what Jesus said in **John 11:25**:
> "Jesus said..., 'I am the resurrection and the life. The one who believes in me will live, even though they die.' "

While it is so sad to know that Granddaddy died, I am so glad to know that he is now in heaven with the Lord Jesus. What a wonderful thing it is to be a Christian!

The part of us that goes to heaven is our **soul**. That is the way God made Adam and Eve. He gave them souls that can never die.

DRAW A CIRCLE AROUND THE ONE
WHICH IS **NOT** TRUE ABOUT THE SOUL?

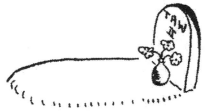

The soul is the part of us that can never die.

The soul goes to live with God forever when the body dies.

Everything that God created has a soul.

God created Adam and Eve with a soul.

Question 19

> **<u>Have you a soul as well as a body</u>**?
> Yes, I have a soul that can never die.

I need your help!

My teacher gave us an assignment to draw ourselves!
What do you look like?
Can you draw yourself?
Don't forget your ears and hands and feet! Remember your mouth and teeth!

DRAW EVERYTHING YOU CAN THINK OF!

Did you draw **all that you can think of**?
Did you draw your **soul**?
What does your soul look like?
Why can't you draw your soul?

Do you know what a soul is?
In our next question,
we are going to find out what a soul is,
and why you can know you have a soul!

Catechism for Young Children

Question 20

How do you know that you have a soul?
Because I can think about God and the world to come.

O, I learned the best hymn today in Sunday School!
I learned it from my teacher. These are the words:

"I think when I read that sweet story of old,
When Jesus was here among men,
How He called little children as Lambs to His fold,
I should like to have been with Him then.

Yet still to His footstool in prayer I may go,
And ask for a share in His love.
And if I thus earnestly seek Him below,
I shall see Him and hear Him above."

Our teacher told us today that we are very different from a plant or from an animal.

Plants and animals and children all are alive. But only a Person has a **soul**.

When God made Adam and Eve, He gave them each a **soul**.

You can read about this in GENESIS 2:7.

There are at least two important reasons why we know we have a **soul**.

The first reason is that **I can think about God**. A plant cannot think about God. An animal cannot think about God. But you can think about God.

The second reason is that **I can think about the world to come**. This means that I can think about heaven. Do you ever think about heaven?

HOW DO YOU KNOW THAT YOU HAVE A SOUL?

1 Because I can think about _____.
2. Because I can think about _____.

Question 21

> **In what condition did God make Adam and Eve**?
> He made them holy and happy.

Hi, Student.

Today I want to share with you a prayer that I prayed one time. I was not a Christian.
I was not even sure that there really was a God who heard me! But I prayed anyway.
My prayer went like this:

"Dear God -- if there is a God -- Would you make me happy? Amen."

I didn't know about the fact that I was a sinner.
I didn't know about the Lord Jesus who died for me.
All I knew was that I wanted to be happy. And if there was a God,
then maybe He could make me happy!

Now when God made Adam and Eve, He made them happy. They were very, very happy.
They had everything that they needed and wanted.

God also made them holy. He made them perfect. There was nothing wrong with them.
To be holy means that they were complete and pure and sinless.

I must confess that when I was praying the prayer above, I wanted to be **happy**, but <u>not</u> **Holy**.
I thought that if I was **Holy** then I could not be **happy**.
I thought that happiness was just having fun all the time!
Happiness is much, much more than just having fun.
Being happy and being holy are like a mother and father.
Mothers and fathers should love each other and be together.
Being happy and being holy go together too!

WHEN GOD MADE ADAM AND EVE,
HE MADE THEM:

_____ and

_____ .

By the way,
do you want to be happy?
Do you want to be holy?

Question 22

> **What is a covenant**?
> An agreement between two or more persons.

This word "**covenant**" is one of the most important words in the Bible!
There are other words that can be used to describe **covenant**.
Some of these words are:

Agreement   **Contract**   **Pledge**   **Compact Promise**

In the answer to our question this week,
a COVENANT is an agreement between _____ or more persons."
It takes at least **two** persons to make a **covenant,** but there may be more.

God is **three persons.**
And you are a **person!**

God can make a **covenant** with **himself** because He is **three persons**!
God can make a **covenant** with **us** because we are **persons!**
And we can make a **covenant** with each other!

In **Genesis**, the first book of the Bible, we see God making several **covenants** with several different men. They were Adam, Noah, and Abraham.

The **covenant** with Adam is called the **covenant of works**. The **covenant** with Noah. is called the **covenant of the rainbow**. The **covenant** with Abraham is called the **Old Covenant**. It is sometimes called the **Covenant of the Old Testament.**

In the lessons to follow, we will learn about **two covenants:**
The covenant of works and the covenant of grace.

TRUE OR FALSE:

A COVENANT IS A <u>DEAL</u>. _____

A COVENANT IS <u>ONLY</u> BETWEEN TWO PERSONS. _____

GOD MADE COVENANTS WITH MEN IN THE OLD TESTAMENT. _____

GOD MADE THE COVENANT OF THE RAINBOW WITH ADAM. _____

Question 23

> ## What covenant did God make with Adam?
> The covenant of works

In the second chapter of Genesis, the first book of the Bible, there is a beautiful account of God making the first man, Adam, and the first woman, Eve. This happened on the sixth day of creation.

Just before God made Eve, He put Adam in a garden. This was the Garden of Eden, a very beautiful garden. Everything that Adam and later, Eve, would need or want could be found in the garden.

Just before God made Eve, He gave clear instructions to Adam on how he was to live in the garden.

You can turn to these instructions in GENESIS 2:15-17. Perhaps your teacher will read these verses aloud to you.

It is very important to understand that Adam was not a **machine**.
He was a **person**. And because he was a **person**, he could make **choices**.
Later, when Eve was made, she also was not a **machine**. She was a **person**.
Because she was a **person**, she could make choices, too.

WHAT DID GOD TELL ADAM THAT HE **COULD DO** IN THE GARDEN?

_____

_____

_____

WHAT DID GOD TELL ADAM THAT HE **WAS NOT TO DO** IN THE GARDEN?

_____

_____

_____

SEE IF YOU CAN UNSCRAMBLE THESE WORDS!

DMAA   _____

WKORS   _____

OGD   _____

KAME   _____

Question 24

> **What was Adam bound to do by the covenant of works?**
> To obey God perfectly.

My dad and I did the neatest thing last summer on our vacation!
We hiked for 50 miles on the Appalachian Trail in North Carolina!
We walked for about 10 miles each day and camped out each night.

Both of us carried back packs.
My dad's backpack was a lot bigger than mine.
On top of the backpack were our sleeping bags.
Inside the backpacks were our food and changes of clothes.

Before we left for our hike, the Park Ranger told us what **not** to do.
He said **not** to leave food out during the night.
He said that the food would attract bears and skunks!

On our first night, after we had bedded down, I heard something.
Very quietly, I turned on my flashlight and saw a **skunk** right beside me!
I had left a candy bar beside my sleeping bag, and he had found it!
But I did remember something: **never** scare a skunk! I didn't move for an hour!

Turn to **GENESIS 2:15-17**, like you did in Question 23.

WHAT WAS THE **ONLY** THING GOD TOLD ADAM **NOT TO DO** IN THE GARDEN?

_____

DO YOU THINK THAT ADAM UNDERSTOOD GOD'S COMMAND? _____
DO YOU THINK THAT GOD WAS BEING TOO MEAN BY NOT LETTING ADAM EAT
THE FRUIT OF THE TREE OF THE KNOWLEDGE OF GOOD AND EVIL?

_____

Question 25

> **What did God promise in the covenant of works**?
> To reward Adam with life is he obeyed Him.

According to Kitty, the kids at her school were wearing some very cool shoes.
"They are the best **sandals** I have ever seen! They come in every color you can imagine! And my mother said I could have a pair!"

Mother agreed to take me to town on Saturday morning to let me pick just the pair I wanted! But on one condition, I was required to **cheerfully** practice the piano **all week.**
So, I **cheerfully** practiced the piano all week long! Now, I really like playing the piano, sometimes it is hard to be **cheerful** when I must practice! However, a deal is a deal, so here is a picture of me trying to look cheerful practicing the piano!

DO YOU SUPPOSE THAT EVE WORE **SANDALS**? _____
What God promised to Adam was far better than sandals.
WHAT DID GOD PROMISE ADAM? _____
WHAT WAS ADAM TO DO? _____
WHAT WAS ADAM <u>NOT</u> TO DO?_____

(YOU WILL NEED TO TURN BACK TO QUESTION 24 TO COPY THE ANSWER.)

_____

_____

_____

_____

Question 26

> ## What did God threaten in the covenant of works?
> To punish Adam with death if he disobeyed.

Have you ever had to housebreak your pet?
Our pet is very hard to housebreak!
If it is raining outside, he does not want to do his "business" outside!
He would rather use the living room carpet! He is a very stubborn pet!
We have threatened him with many punishments.
    Sometimes he listens. Sometimes he doesn't.
We threaten him with the newspaper.
We threaten him with a long stay in the basement.
We threaten him with making him stay outside all night.
    Sometimes he obeys. Sometimes he doesn't.

Do you know what **threaten** means? Let's look it up!

THREATEN

_____

_____

TURN ONCE AGAIN TO GENESIS 2:15-17. In verse 17, write down God's threat to Adam (Only the last half of the verse!)

_____

_____

READ **GENESIS 5:5** AND FIND OUT IF GOD KEPT HIS THREAT TO ADAM.

HOW OLD WAS ADAM WHEN HE DIED?
____ YEARS OLD.

(By the way, Kitty will introduce you to our pet in Question 36!)

Question 27

> **Did Adam keep the covenant of works**?
> No, he sinned against God.

In **Matthew 21:28-31**, Jesus told a story. It goes like this:

"There was a man  who had [ ] [ ] [ ]. The man went

to the first and said, 'Son, go and work today in the vineyard.'

'I will not!' [ ] he answered, but later changed his mind and went.

"Then the father went to the other son and [ ] said the same thing.

'Son, go and work today in the vineyard. Son. His son answered, 'I will, Sir' But, he did <u>not</u> go.

"Which of the two did what the father wanted?" asked Jesus.

When I read about the story of Adam's refusal to obey God, I imagine that he was like the second son in the story above.

I can imagine God saying to Adam,

"Now Adam, do not eat of the tree in the middle of the garden. If you do, you will die. Adam, do you understand?"

And I can imagine Adam saying:

"O yes, God, I understand. I understand that I am not to eat of the tree in the middle of the garden. I will die if I do. O yes, I understand."

And then Adam chose to disobey God even though he understood God's command.

Question 28

What is sin?
Sin is any want of conformity unto, or transgression of, the law of God.

When we get to Questions 72-104, we will study what we call the Ten Commandments.

The Ten Commandments were given by God to a man named Moses. In this way, God was teaching His people how they were to live with Him and with each other.

The Ten Commandments are found in **Exodus 20:1-17.** When we read these verses, we realize how far short we come from being perfect. We realize that we really are sinners. In some ways, we do not live as God wants us to live. In some ways, we choose to disobey God.

Your teacher will Read the TEN COMMANDNENTS from EXODUS 20.
SEE IF YOU CAN PUT THEM IN ORDER.

_____ You shall not steal.	_____ Remember the Sabbath day by keeping it holy. Six days you shall labor and do
_____ You shall not misuse the name of the Lord our God, for the Lord will not hold anyone guiltless who misuse his name.	all your work, but the seventh day is a Sabbath to the Lord your God.
	_____ You shall not give false testimony against your neighbor.
_____ You shall not murder.	_____ You shall not covet.
_____ You shall have no other Gods before Me.	_____ You shall not commit adultery.
_____ You shall not make for yourself an idol in the form of anything in heaven above or on the earth beneath or in the waters below.	_____ Honor your father and your mother, so that you may live long in the land the Lord your God is giving you.

Did you get them all in order?
The Bible says that all of us have broken these
Ten Commandments.
Just like arrows which fall short of the target,
we fall short of God's plan for us.

Question 29

What is meant by want of conformity?
Not being or doing what God requires.

We have a new girl in our school. Her name is Candie Sweet Thing.
She is already really popular. Her clothes are just so cool.
Her hair is just the right style. In fact, every girl in our class wants to be just like Candie!

This is what **conformity** means.
It means to "act alike" or "be alike."

Our Heavenly Father wants us to **conform**, too.
But He wants us to **conform** to something more important than clothes or hairstyles.

Our heavenly Father wants us to be like the Lord Jesus.
Does this mean I have to wear long clothes like He did?
Or that I have to grow a beard? That would be funny to see all of us in beards!

But that's not what God wants.
He wants us to be like the Lord Jesus in our hearts.
We are to be like Him in our **attitudes**. We are to treat others the way He treats them.

See if you can MATCH the GOOD ATTITUDE with the BAD ATTITUDE.
To which ATTITUDES are we to CONFORM?

Joy	Cruelty
Patience	Impatience
Gentleness	Disagreeable
Kindness	Miserable

When we do not **conform** to the attitudes on the left, then we have sinned.
Do you **always conform** to the **good attitudes**?

Question 30

> **What is meant by transgression**?
> Doing what God forbids.

Do you play sports for your school or in the City Recreation League? Both Kitty and I do! Kitty plays on the City Recreation Softball team, and I play soccer and run track in school. Playing sports with others is a great way to be with others and also keep your body in shape!

The other day at a track meet, I was in two events, the Pole Vault, and the Hurdles. I hope you know that rules for the Pole Vaulting and rules for Hurdles are different. One of the main differences is that in the Hurdles, a person runs on the track and jumps a row of hurdles as he runs. But in the Pole Vault, the person has a long pole which he uses the get himself over a very high bar.

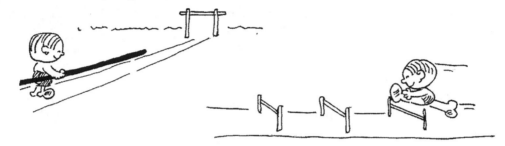

It would be funny to try to run **Hurdles** with a **Pole Vault**! Not only would it be funny, but the **rules** would not let me! The judges would throw me out!
I must play the game according to the RULES of Track and Field! Kitty has to play her games by the soft ball rules.

God's Word is like a **Rule Book**.
God's Word tells us how we are to live our lives. And when we don't follow God's Word, we sin.

LOOK IT UP

Look up COLOSSIANS 3:20. Fill in the missing words.

"_____, obey your _____ in everything, for this _____ the Lord."

WHAT DOES GOD FORBID IN THIS VERSE? _____

_____

When we do what God tells us **not** to do, then we sin.

Question 31

What was the sin of our first parents?
Eating the forbidden fruit.

COMPLETE THE SENTENCES BELOW
The first two people God made were _____ and _____.
God made the body of _____ out of the _____, and formed
_____ from
the body of _____. What else did God give these first two people besides bodies?

Hey, student, if you did those last seven blanks without looking at your Catechism, then you
did really well! **Great**! You are learning these truths of the Bible. Keep hanging in there!

When God made Adam and Eve, He put them in the most wonderful place that you can
imagine. This place was called the Garden of Eden. Everything they needed, God provided.

All the food they wanted was there for them to eat.
The weather was always good. The animals were their friends.
And God Himself came to be with them at the close of each day. What more could they want?

There was only one thing that God told Adam and Eve not to do: to leave one tree-- only one
tree-- and its fruit **alone**!

TURN IN YOUR BIBLE TO GENESIS 3:6.
Did Adam and Eve obey God? _____

What did they do? _____

_____

What was the name of the tree they ate from? You can look up its name in Genesis 2:15-17.

It is quite a lo-o-o-o-ng name! _____

Question 32

┌───┐
│ <u>**Who tempted them to this sin?**</u>   │
│ The devil tempted Eve, and she gave the fruit to Adam. │
└───┘

My sister, Kitty, is so sad today. She is so sad because of what happened to Adam and Eve. You can read the story which has made her sad in **Genesis 3: 8-13.**

AFTER READING THIS STORY, REMEMBER THAT IT IS A TRUE STORY! READ THE STORY, THEN **CIRCLE THE WORD** THAT DESCRIBES YOUR FEELINGS ABOUT WHAT ADAM AND EVE DID.

Happy   Sad   Mad   Ho-Hum   Surprised

Do you know what that word "**tempted**" means?
It means "that something that is bad for us look like it is good."

The devil made disobeying God look good to Adam and Eve.

Now I want you to read what happened after Adam and Eve disobeyed God.
READ **GENESIS 3:8-13**.

Whom did Adam blame for disobeying God? **Genesis 3:12** _____

Whom did Eve blame for disobeying God? **Genesis 3: 13** _____

Do you ever blame others when you disobey your parents? _____

Do you ever blame others when you disobey your teacher? _____

Whenever you are **tempted** to disobey, maybe you should do what the little boy did in this story:

Once upon a time (this is a make-pretend story!), a little boy was having trouble obeying his mother. One day his father told him, "Son, the next time the devil comes knocking at your heart's door and tempts you to disobey Mother, ask the Lord Jesus to answer the door. When the devil sees that the Lord Jesus is living in your heart, he will run away!"

Student, the next time the devil knocks at your heart's door and tempts you to do wrong, ask the Lord Jesus to answer the door!

Question 33

> <u>**What befell our first parents when they had sinned?**</u>
> Instead of being holy and happy, they became sinful and miserable.

Hi!

IV said that I could teach the lesson today, and I am so excited! Sometimes Big Brothers do not think that Little Sisters can do anything!

Today we are going to learn what a **contrast** is. Have you ever heard that word? It means **two different things**, or sometimes, **opposite things**.

What would be the **contrast** of **light?**
(You are right! It is **dark**!)

NOW TRY TO MATCH THESE CONTRASTS:

God	**Night**
Adam	**Sinful**
Day	**Devil**
Holy	**Eve**
Happy	**Miserable**

That wasn't too hard, was it?

You remember that Adam and Eve were created or made to be **holy** and **happy**.
To be **holy** meant that there was no sin in their lives or hearts.
After they disobeyed God, they became sinners. Because they were now sinners, they became **miserable**.

To be miserable did not mean that they were always sad and crying.
It meant that they would never again know the happiness and joy they once had.
It also meant that one day they were going to die.

 Now I want you to get your Bible. Please look up **Genesis 3:8.**
Adam and Eve were so **miserable** after they disobeyed God.
What did they do when they heard God walking in the garden in the cool of the day?

_____

Question 38

<u>Can anyone go to heaven with this sinful nature?</u>
No, our hearts must be changed before we can be fit for heaven.

The other day my mother asked me to go to the grocery store with her.
Our grocer's name is Mr. Ralph. His grocery is just a block from our house.
It is a small store, but Mr. Ralph sells many different things.
He sells meats, fruit, vegetables, milk, and a of variety other things.

I hope all of us know how each kind of food looks.
Below are pictures of **meat** and **fruit** and **milk** and **bread**.
Can you tell the difference in each?

_____   _____   _____   _____

I bet you weren't fooled. You can tell the difference, can't you?
Did you know that God cannot be fooled either?
He knows who is His child and who is not.
He knows if you are a Christian, or if you are not.

I want you to think about a question.

"If you were to die tonight and were to appear before God in heaven, and if God were to ask
you, **"Why should I let you into my heaven?"** what do you think you would say to Him?

If you were to say, **"Because I have been good,"**
God would say that your heart has not be changed.

If you were to say, **"My mother and daddy are Christians,"**
God would say that your heart has not been changed.

If you were to say, **"I go to church every Sunday,"**
God would say that your heart has not been changed.

All these things-- **Being Good,**
 Having Christian parents,
 Going to church are very good things.

However, only a changed heart will get you into heaven. Only God can change your heart.

Question 39

> ### What is a change of heart called?
> Regeneration.

If our last lesson, we talked about how our hearts must be changed before we can be fit for heaven.

My brother, IV, has decided to let me tell you about the **heart** today. He says that girls know more about the **heart** and mushy love and valentines and all that, than boys do.

Well, what IV does not know is that when the Bible talks about the **heart**, it is not talking about "mushy love and valentines and all that."

When the Bible talks about the **heart**, it is talking about the **real me**. The part of me that loves and hates, is happy or is sad, and has feelings and desires, is my **heart**.

Do you remember my cat?
DO YOU REMEMBER WHAT HIS NAME IS?

_____

I have a friend named Molly.
Molly has a dog.
Her dog's name is Bugs.
My cat and Molly's dog are very much alike. They each have four legs, whiskers, and a tail. But they are different, not only in looks, but in what they really are. You might say Saltine has a **cat's heart** and Bugs has a **dog's heart**.

Now I have a **heart** too. But it is not a cat's heart, and it is not a dog's heart. It is a **girl's heart**. That means that I feel and act, and love and hate, and am sad and happy like a **girl**.

But I also am a **sinner**. My heart is a **sinner's heart**.
And my heart needs to be changed before I can go to heaven.

WHAT IS THIS CHANGE OF HEART CALLED? _____

In our next question, we are going to find out how we can have our hearts changed so that we can go to heaven.

Question 40

<u>Who can change a sinner's heart?</u> The Holy Spirit alone.

Today we are going to try to guess what these **silhouettes** are!
Do you know what a **silhouette** is? It is an outline picture in black.
What are these? There is a **horse** and a **bat**,

a **porcupine** and a **cat**,
a **kangaroo** and a **rat**,
a **dog** and a **what is that**?

CAN YOU
POINT TO
THESE
ANIMALS?

The Bible talks about another
kind of animal when it talks
about a change of heart.

LOOK UP JEREMIAH 13:23
IN THE OLD TESTAMENT
AND WRITE IT DOWN.

_____

_____

_____

_____

I cannot change the color of my skin. A leopard cannot change its spots.
And I cannot change my sinful **heart**. Only the Holy Spirit can change my **heart**.

The Holy Spirit comes into our **hearts** when we ask Him to come
in. He makes us Christians
He cleanses our **hearts** from sin and gives us a **love** for God and
for one another.

Question 41

Can anyone be saved through the covenant of works?
None can be saved through the covenant of works.

Today, student, we need to do a little backtracking. Backtracking is when you go back over a course or path. Today we need to remind ourselves of what a **covenant** is and what the **covenant of works** was.

WHAT IS A COVENANT?

_____

It would be good for you to review Catechism questions 23-27.

    WHAT COVENANT DID GOD MAKE WITH ADAM?
    WHAT WAS ADAM BOUND TO DO BY THE COVENANT OF WORKS?
    WHAT DID GOD PROMISE IN THE COVENANT OF WORKS?
    WHAT DID GOD THREATEN IN THE COVENANT OF WORKS?
    DID ADAM KEEP THE COVENANT OF WORKS?

You can look back in your Workbook to Question 31 for these answers.

ADAM AND EVE HAD TWO CHOICES IN THE GARDEN. WHAT WERE THEY?

_____

Or

_____

You remember that Adam chose to disobey God, and he died.
First, he died on the inside-- he no longer wanted to love God.
And then, years and years later, he died on the outside.

Since God made the **covenant of works only** with Adam, no one else can be saved by it. God did not make the **covenant of works** with anyone else.

WITH WHOM DID GOD MAKE THE COVENANT OF WORKS? _____

DID GOD MAKE THE COVENANT OF WORKS WITH ANYONE ELSE _____

HOW MANY PERSONS HAVE BEEN SAVED BY THE COVENANT OF WORKS?_____

Question 42

<u>Why can none be saved through the covenant of works?</u>
Because all have broken it and are condemned by it.

On our last Question we did some backtracking with Questions 22-27. Sometimes it is fun to backtrack and sometimes it isn't. But it is important so that you remind yourself of what you have learned. Sometimes we forget and need to review (backtrack!).

TODAY LET'S GO BACK TO JUST FIVE QUESTIONS-- 34-38. READ, THINK, CHECK

Did Adam act for himself alone in the covenant of works?
What effect had the sin of Adam on all mankind?
What is that sinful nature which we inherit from Adam called?
What does every sin deserve?
Can anyone go to heaven with this sinful nature?

Did you remember all the answers to all these questions! Do you remember Question 21?

IN WHAT CONDITION DID GOD MAKE ADAM AND EVE? _____

_____

(Did you remember that this was Question 21?)

When God made Adam and Eve, they did not know what sin was because they had never sinned. But when Adam chose to disobey God, he sinned, and everyone born from Adam and Eve were born as sinners. We cannot get into heaven by being good because we are sinners.

One summer I went to Camp. One of the things I learned was **archery**. It looked so easy until I tried it! My arrows were shot from my bow with careful aim, but for the first few days my arrows never reached the target. They fell far short of it!

As sinners, we fall far short of what God has for us. We cannot go to heaven by our own good works because they never are good enough!

WRITE OUT ROMANS 3:23.

_____

_____

_____

Question 43

> <u>**With whom did God the Father make the covenant of grace?**</u>
> With Christ, His eternal Son.

I have just finished reading a great book! It is *The Lion, the Witch, and the Wardrobe* by C.S. Lewis.

It is the story about four children-- Peter, Susan, Edmund, and Lucy-- and their adventures in a land named Narnia. It is about a wicked, wicked Witch and a fantastic lion named **Aslan**.

At one point in the story, one of the children, Edmund, becomes a traitor and is to die. But **Aslan** takes his place and dies for him. Here is how the story goes:

> "When once **Aslan** had been tied (and tied so that he was really a mass of cords) on the flat stone, a hush fell on the crowd. The Witch bared her arms. Then she began to whet her knife. It looked to the children, when the gleam of the torchlight fell on it, as if the knife were made of stone not of steel, and it was of a strange and evil shape. At last she drew near. She stood by **Aslan's** head. Her face was working and twitching with passion, but he looked up at the sky, still quiet, neither angry nor afraid, but a little sad. Then, just before she gave the blow, she stooped down and said in a quivering voice, 'And now, who has won? Fool, did you think that by all this you would save the human traitor? Now I will kill you instead of him as our pact was and so the Deep Magic will be appeased.' The children did not see the actual moment of the killing. They couldn't bear to look and had covered their eyes."
> And so, **Aslan** died for Edmund.

God is a Trinity-- Father, Son, and Holy Spirit.
God is **holy** and He cannot let us into heaven because we are sinners.
But God loves us so much that He-- God, the Son-- came to take our place, to die for us so that we could go to heaven.

ADAM REPRESENTED US IN THE COVENANT OF _____.

CHRIST REPRESENTED US IN THE COVENANT OF _____.

The covenant of works?   The covenant of Grace?

Catechism for Young Children

Question 44

> **Whom did Christ represent in the covenant of grace?**
> His elect people.

One of the most exciting things I do each day is **Bible study**! God's Word says that if I love Him then I will obey Him. And I can only obey Him if I know His Word! So you can see, it is very important to read and study God's Word! We are going to look at just two verses of God's Word and try to understand what "**elect**" means.

In I Peter 1:1, 2 we read, "**To God's elect, strangers in the world, scattered …. who have been chosen according to the foreknowledge of God the Father, through the sanctifying work of the spirit, for obedience to Jesus Christ and sprinkling by his blood.**"

NOW LET'S FILL IN THE BLANKS:

TO GOD'S,_____

Who have been _____ according to the foreknowledge

of God the _____, through the sanctifying work

of the _____ for

_____ to Jesus Christ and sprinkling by His blood."

According to God's Word, **you** are one of God's **elect people** if you have been **chosen** by God. The way that you can know if you have been **chosen** by God is to ask yourself these questions:

1. **Am I trusting in Christ alone to save me?** Have I been cleansed by His blood? He has sent His Son who lived, taught us, died for us. We say, "Yes!"

2. **Am I walking in obedience to his word daily?** Do you want to do God's will day by day?

Student, it is so important to say YES! to these two questions-- not only with your **mouth** but, more importantly, with your **heart**. God sees us. He hears. He knows!

Question 45

> <u>**What did Christ undertake in the covenant of grace?**</u>
> To keep the whole law for His people, and to suffer the punishment due to their sins.

When Jesus was born in a manger in Bethlehem, He came to do two very, very important things.

1. He came to live a perfect life for us. You will remember that in the covenant of works, Adam failed to obey God and fell. Adam never lived a perfect life. Jesus did.

2. Jesus also came to die for our sins. Because we are sinners, we deserve to go to hell. But God loved us so much that He sent His Son to take the punishment of our sins upon Himself. And because He died for us, if we trust in Him alone for salvation, we will go to heaven when we die!

Jesus' **life** and **death** (and **resurrection**!) are very important!
Maybe we can understand it better if I tell you a story:

You owe $1000 to Mean Old Oscar Screwface! If you don't pay by noon tomorrow, Oscar is going to take your 10-speed bike that has only one speed, Your yo-yo without a string, and your dolly whose eyes are punched out. However, you don't have $1000!

But…wonder of wonders! All of sudden, Miss Mary Blue-Fairy flies in and gives you a $1000. Now you can pay Mean old Oscar Screwface!

But wait! Miss Mary Blue Fairy gives You another $1,000!!

You not only can pay Oscar the $1,000 you owe him, but you have Another $1,000 to buy a brand new 10-speed bike (with 12 speeds!), a new purple yo-yo, and a dolly with one beautiful green eye in the middle of her forehead!

When the Lord Jesus dies for you, He washed away all of your sins. But with His perfect life, you are now clothed in His righteousness And are fit for heaven.

You now live with your sins forgiven and clothed in the righteousness of Jesus!

Can you tell me what two things Jesus has done for you?

Question 46

> **<u>Did our Lord Jesus Christ ever commit the least sin?</u>**
> No, He was holy, harmless, and undefiled.

IV and I are mad at each other. He said that it was my turn to feed Saltine. But it was his turn! Our mom said that while we are arguing and being mad at each other, Saltine is still hungry! But it's not my turn to feed him!

Later, IV was so sweet. He fed Saltine. I am so sorry for the way I acted. IV and I apologized.

When the Lord Jesus was born in Bethlehem so many years ago, He was born and lived **holy**, **harmless**, and **undefiled.**

LET'S GET A DICTIONARY AND LOOK UP THOSE WORDS. If you are working on this question in a group, maybe you can divide your group into three small groups and have each group look up a word. Then each group can report to the other two.

HOLY

HARMLESS

UNDEFILED

The Lord Jesus never once sinned.

Can you imagine never once sinning? Never disobeying your mom or dad? Always loving those around you… even your enemies? Never once, saying or doing an unkind thing to someone else? This is hard to imagine, but this was how Jesus was born and lived!

Question 47

How could the Son of God suffer?
Christ, the Son of God, became man that He might obey and suffer in our nature.

Do you have a nickname?
Does your mom call you something that no one else does? Like Sweetie?
Does your dad call you something that shows how much he Like "Bubba?"
Maybe your teacher calls you a nickname.
And maybe your classmates call you a nickname.
These names are very special and tells others how much you mean to them.

When the Lord Jesus lived on the earth there were two names He was called. One is the "Son of God," and the other is the "Son of Man."

The name, "Son of God," means that Jesus was the only begotten Son of God. He is the eternal Son of God. This name means that He is God, the Second Person of the Trinity.

The name, "Son of Man," means that He was also truly man. As a man, He could take our place. He could suffer for us. As a man, as a perfect man, He could learn what it means suffer and die.

As a man, He also learned how to obey.
TURN IN YOUR BIBLE TO HEBREWS 5:8 AND READ THIS VERSE.

WHO IS IT TALKING ABOUT? _____

WHAT DOES IT SAY HE LEARNED? _____

HOW DID HE LEARN IT? _____

The Lord Jesus has other names which are:

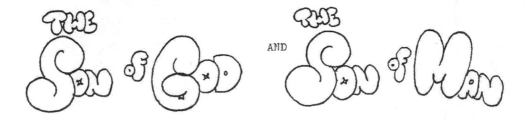

Question 48

> ## What is meant by the atonement?
> Christ's satisfying divine justice by His sufferings and death, in the place of sinners.

Atonement-- Can you say this word? If you say it by syllables, you can tell what it means!

We have studied several new words in the Catechism, words like "**covenant**," and "**glorify**," and "**regeneration**." This is another new word, "**atonement**." What does it mean?

Perhaps we can show what it means. Try to imagine two cliffs with a deep, deep, wide, wide chasm separating them. We are on one side, and God is on the other. The deep chasm is **sin** which separates us from God.

The Son of God bridges the chasm by His death for us on the cross.

If we will trust Him, we will "walk over" the bridge to God's side. We will then become a part of God's **forever family**.

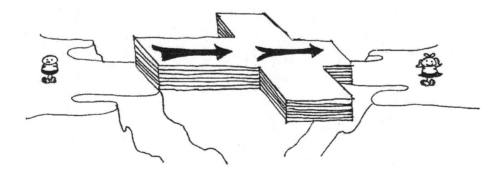

If you break up this word, "**atonement**," you will understand it better. Through Christ's death on the cross, we are "**at-one**" with our heavenly Father. All of our sins are forgiven.

Question 49

> **What did God the Father undertake in the covenant of grace?**
> To justify and sanctify those for whom Christ should die.

Have you ever had a **sword drill**? Now I don't mean the kind with real swords! A **sword drill** is when each student has a closed Bible. The teacher calls out a Bible verse twice and then says, "**Charge!**" After the word "**charge**," whoever finds the verse first wins.

IN THE **SWORD DRILL** TODAY YOU WILL SEE A WORD REPEATED OVER AND OVER AGAIN IN ALL SIX VERSES. SEE IF YOU CAN PICK IT OUT!

Here are the verses your teacher will call out: JOHN 3:16   ROMANS 5:8
                                              JOHN 14:23   II CORINTHIANS 13:14
                                              JOHN 15:9   I JOHN 4:16
                                                           (Now close your Bible and GO!)

WHY DID GOD THE FATHER SEND HIS SON TO DIE FOR US? Answer below!

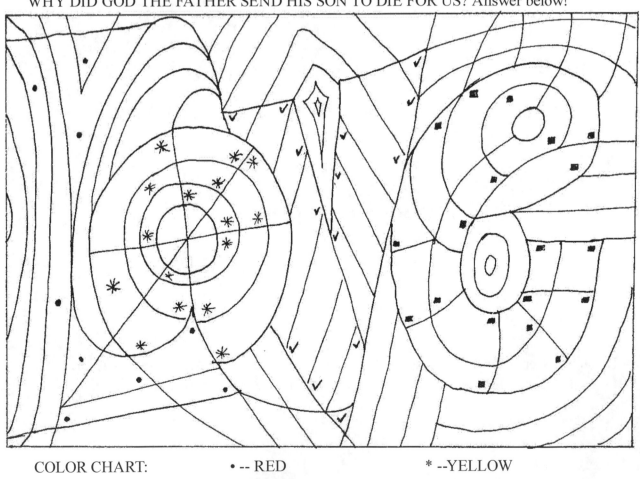

COLOR CHART: • -- RED   * --YELLOW
                      ✓ --GREEN   ■ --ORANGE

Question 50

> **What is justification?**
> It is God's forgiving sinners and treating them as if they had never sinned.

I like **Happily-Ever-After** stories, don't you? My daddy has been reading some Fairy Tales to me, and I love them! He read me a fairy tale last night called *"Rapunzel."*
It is about a beautiful young woman named Rapunzel. She is trapped in a tall tower by a mean, wicked witch. There are no doors into the tower. The only way to get to Rapunzel's room at the top is to call,

> "Rapunzel, Rapunzel,
> Let down your hair."

Rapunzel's hair is very, very long. She lets her hair out the window, and the witch climbs up her hair and into the tower. The story is so sad, but it ends "**Happily-Ever-After**." Of course a prince saves Rapunzel.

All Rapunzel's sadness is Just-As-If it had never happened!

Now when the Lord Jesus died for me, it was **no** fairy tale! It really happened!

When I invite the Lord Jesus into my life, many things happen. First, my sins are **forgiven**! **All** of my sins are **forgiven**!

And then God treats me as if I had never sinned. That's how you can remember what **justification** means. God treats me "**just-as-if-I'd**" never sinned!

LOOK UP **JEREMIAH 31:34**. HOW DOES GOD REMEMBER OUR SINS?

N _____   M _____!

Question 51

> **What is sanctification?**
> It is God's making sinners holy in heart and conduct.

Last summer in Vacation Bible School, our teacher told us a story.
It is a story about Mrs. O'Leary and her **pig**!

Once upon a time, Mrs. O'Leary had a cute, sweet pig.
But, oh, was the pig dirty!
That pig loved mud puddles!

One day Mrs. O'Leary decided enough was enough! She was going to bathe her pig.
She scrubbed and scrubbed and scrubbed. Her pig came out clean and pink.
The pig turned out so shiny and pink that Mrs. O'Leary decided to put a pink bow on the pig!
The bow looked so good that Mrs. O'Leary put the pig on the living room couch.
When Mrs. O'Leary went to get her pig some lunch and came back, the pig was gone!
Mrs. O'Leary looked all over for the pig.
Where do you think she finally found her pig? Right! Back in the mud puddle!
No matter how clean and shiny and pretty and pink the pig was, the pig still had a pig's heart.
And a pig's heart loves the mud.

When God forgives us and washes us clean of all our sins, He does something more. He begins to make us ready for heaven.

He does this in two ways.
First of all, He begins to make us **holy** in our **hearts**. That is, He gives us a special desire in our hearts to want to please Him.

The second way He makes us ready for heaven is that He begins to make us holy in our conduct, or the way we act. When you love a person, you want to please that person. And because you want to please him, you will begin to do special loving things for him.

CAN YOU THINK OF SOME WAYS THAT GOD MAKES US HOLY IN OUR CONDUCT?

Question 52

> **<u>For whom did Christ obey and suffer?</u>**
> For those whom the Father had given Him.

Wow! The question today is a hard one!
But I want you to do some digging-- some **Bible Digging**!
You know if you have a little brother or sister that he or she does not eat the same things that they did when they were first born.
When a baby is new-born, the baby drinks **milk**.
As the baby gets older, the baby is able to eat **solid food**.
And when the baby is no longer a baby, then he or she eats **meat**-- like steak!

So today we are going to have some **solid food**-- and to some of us it will be **meat**-- like steak!

DO YOU REMEMBER THE ANSWER TO THE CATECHISM QUESTION #44? **WHOM DID CHRIST REPRESENT IN THE COVENANT OF GRACE?**

_____

When the Lord Jesus died, He died for all people.
But in a very, very special way, He died **especially for the elect**.

I WANT YOU TO LOOK UP AND WRITE OUT TWO VERSES AND THEN
TALK ABOUT WHAT THEY MEAN WITH YOUR TEACHER AND YOUR CLASS.

John 6:37 _____

_____

_____

John 17:9 _____

_____

_____

HOW WOULD YOU KNOW THAT YOU ARE ONE OF GOD'S CHOSEN ONES?
ACCORDING TO **JOHN 6:37** WHAT MUST WE DO TO BE SURE THAT WE ARE ONE
OF GOD'S CHOSEN ONES?

_____

Question 53

<u>What kind of life did Christ live on earth?</u> A life of poverty and suffering.

Last Sunday our pastor told us about a man whose name is Haralan Popov. Popov is a Christian who grew up in the country of Bulgaria. Bulgaria is right next to Russia and is a Communist country. Haralan Popov was very poor. In a book, *Tortured for His Faith*, he describes his home when he was a little boy:

"I was born and spent my youth in the beautiful little town of Krasnov Gradate, in Bulgaria. There were four of us children, three brothers and a sister. We were born in an old Turkish-built farmhouse, consisting of one room and a kitchen. The ceiling was so low that my father had to duck so as not to hit his head on the beams above. The house had a dirt floor, which mother painted with a mixture of manure, clay, and water. It didn't smell very nice, but it was a disinfectant, and the manure kept the floor from cracking.

"We all slept in one room, on the floor covered with rugs made of plaited reeds. On one side of the kitchen was the large, blackened fireplace on which stood an array of sooty, cracked clay pots...

"...Even though we were very poor, my parents managed to send me to a little school in a nearby village. They were very proud of my ability to read and did all they could to continue my education. I began attending school dressed in patched, home-woven clothes and homemade moccasin-like shoes made of raw pigskin, with the big bristles turned out. I looked a sight!...

"I had my first pair of proper shoes when I was 17."

It is very hard to imagine that you would be so poor that you would make your shoes out of pigskin or that you would have to paint your floor with manure!

Many people in our world today are so poor that they do not have homes or beds to sleep in. They sleep on the streets and in the gutters along the roadside.

The Lord Jesus was poor too. When He was born, He was put in a cow's feeding trough. When He grew up the only clothes He had were the ones He wore. And He didn't have any place to sleep each night!

But there was a very special reason for His being so poor.
LOOK UP THIS REASON IN **II CORINTHIANS 8:9** AND WRITE IT DOWN.

"...THOUGH HE WAS RICH

_____."

Catechism for Young Children

Question 54

> ## What kind of death did Christ die?
> The painful and shameful death of the cross.

Do you know <u>why</u> Jesus died on the cross?
The cross was the most horrible kind of death that the Romans inflicted. I don't even want to describe it. It was so very bad!

But Jesus died on the cross for a purpose.

IF YOU WILL LOOK UP IN YOUR BIBLE **JOHN 3:16** YOU WILL SEE WHY!
I know that some of you know that verse by heart!
But look it up anyway and copy it down!

JOHN 3:16 _____

_____

_____

_____

Here is a Bible-verse puzzle! Every word in JOHN 3:16 is in the puzzle. See if you can find all the words!

E	E	A	C	E	H	I	K	M	S	W	M
V	B	H	D	G	F	T	J	I	N	H	L
E	H	G	F	S	I	L	H	O	P	O	K
R	T	T	F	O	R	S	R	E	Q	S	J
L	A	H	E	D	C	G	T	G	U	O	I
A	H	A	X	A	B	A	W	O	V	E	H
S	T	T	V	L	O	V	E	D	X	V	B
T	O	U	W	Y	Z	E	Y	A	Z	E	U
I	N	D	L	R	O	W	B	H	L	R	T
N	O	N	Q	S	N	O	C	I	E	F	G
G	M	P	T	R	L	D	E	M	O	P	N
L	S	O	N	E	Y	V	S	R	E	Q	E
J	I	H	D	W	E	U	T	F	I	R	V
K	G	C	X	T	T	V	I	B	D	S	A
F	B	S	H	O	U	L	D	E	C	A	H
A	Z	Y	N	E	T	T	O	G	E	B	F

I just know that the girls find every word of verse in the puzzle! Maybe the boys will, too!

Question 55

> **<u>Who will be saved?</u>**
> Only those who repent of sin, believe in Christ, and lead holy lives.

YOUR TEACHER WILL READ **MATTHEW 19:16-22** TO YOU.
READ THE STORY BELOW AND PUT THE CORRECT WORDS IN THE BLANKS.
These are the words:

Great	**Commandments**	**Life**
Give	**Follow**	**Poor**
Kept	**Sad**	**Heaven**
Loved		

A Long Time Ago, when the Lord Jesus was living here on the earth, a young man came to Him. This young man was very rich. But there was one thing that he did not have. Not even money could buy this for him. He did not have eternal _____.

"What good deed can I do to have eternal life?" the young man asked Jesus.

"If you want eternal life, you must keep all of God's_____," Jesus told him.

"But I have _____ these since I was a little boy." the rich young man replied. "What else must I do?"

Now Jesus knew that the young man _____ his riches more than he loved God.

"Then," said Jesus, "sell all that you have and _____ it to the _____, and come and _____ Me."

The young man was very _____ for he had _____ wealth. But he would not obey the Lord Jesus.

The Lord Jesus was telling the young man to repent of loving his riches more than he loved God. The Lord Jesus was telling the young man to trust in the Lord more than he was trusting in his money. But the young man would not obey because he loved his money more than he loved God.

READ VERSE 21 AGAIN AND ANSWER THIS: Where would the young man's treasure have been if he had obeyed the Lord Jesus?

_____

Catechism for Young Children

Question 56

| **What is it to repent?** |
| To be sorry for sin, and to hate and forsake it, because it is displeasing to God. |

Do you remember the answer to the Catechism Question 55?
WHO WILL BE SAVED?
Only those who   1. _____
                 2. _____
     and   3. _____

TODAY I WANT YOU TO TURN IN YOUR BIBLE TO **LUKE 15:11-24**.
Perhaps you can see what it is to repent, if you read about a young man who did just that!

WHO TOLD THIS STORY? _____

THIS IS A STORY ABOUT A MAN AND HIS _____
WHAT DID THE YOUNGER SON ASK OF HIS FATHER?_____
_____

WHAT DID THE YOUNGER SON DO WITH THE MONEY HIS FATHER GAVE HIM?
_____

_____

Now, you are going to really have to put on your thinking caps to answer these next questions!

DID THE YOUNG MAN REPENT? _____

HOW DO YOU KNOW HE REPENTED?

     WAS HE SORRY FOR HIS SIN? _____

     DID HE HATE WHAT HE HAD DONE WRONG? _____

     DID HE FORSAKE HIS SIN?

In class you need to point out from the Bible exactly how you know the young man repented.

BY THE WAY, WHAT WAS THE YOUNG MAN'S SIN?

Question 57

> ### What is it to believe or have faith in Christ?
> To trust in Christ alone for salvation.

Several years ago my family went to **Mexico**.
Kitty and I met many new friends. Our new friends speak Spanish.
We didn't understand each other too well, but we still had fun!

We met a beautiful lady whose name is Vickie Victoria. Her husband is a Mexican doctor, and they have nine children!

She told us how she became a Christian.
She said that before she became a Christian she went to Church.
She said that before she became a Christian she prayed.
She said that before she became a Christian she was baptized.
She said that before she became a Christian, she helped others.
However, she was not a Christian. She did not look to the
Lord Jesus as her Lord, as the One who forgave her sins.
She said that she knew she was not going to heaven when she died.
One day God led her to a Bible study.

It was at Bible study that she realized that she was not trusting in Christ alone for her salvation. She was trusting in how good she was! After the Bible study that afternoon, she asked the Lord Jesus into her life-- she began to trust Christ alone for salvation.

Now Vickie Victoria still goes to Church. She still prays. She still helps others...
   but she does all these things **because** she loves the Lord Jesus!

WHAT WERE THE THINGS VICKIE VICTORIA WAS TRUSTING IN?

1. _____

2. _____

3. _____

4. _____

CAN ANYONE GO TO HEAVEN JUST BY DOING ALL THESE THINGS?_____

_____

HOW DOES A PERSON GO TO HEAVEN?_____

_____

Question 58

<u>**Can you repent and believe in Christ by your own power?**</u> No; I can do nothing good without the help of God's Holy Spirit.

In order to do this question, you are going to have to review!
GO WAY, WAY BACK TO QUESTIONS 7 AND 8.
READ OVER THEM AND THEN ANSWER THESE QUESTIONS:

IN HOW MANY PERSONS DOES THIS ONE GOD EXIST?

_____

WHAT ARE THEY?

_____

WHAT DO THESE SYMBOLS REPRESENT?

_____   _____

_____   _____

LOOK UP **LUKE 3:21, 22.** WHAT IS THE SYMBOL FOR THE HOLY SPIRIT?

When the Holy Spirit makes us into God's children, He then begins to help us <u>act</u> as His children.

Perhaps some people say you look like your daddy.
Perhaps some people say you look like your mother.

Perhaps you do not look like them at all!
Perhaps you act like them!

When we become God's special children, we do not **look** like Him.
But we are to begin to **act** like Him!

And this is how the Holy Spirit helps us.
We will see in our next question just how He helps us!

Catechism for Young Children

Question 59

> ### How can you get the help of the Holy Spirit?
> God has told us that we must pray to Him for the Holy Spirit.

Even though IV and I are in different grades in school,
we still help each other with our homework.
I am good in math,
and IV is good in spelling.

Whenever I have trouble with my spelling,
I ask IV to help me. He does!
Whenever he has a problem with his math,
he asks me to help him. And I do!

It is a real joy to help someone when they ask for help.

When you become a Christian, it is because
the Holy Spirit has come into your life and
given you faith to trust the Lord Jesus as your
Lord and Savior.

As you begin to live as a Christian, the Holy
Spirit lives in you and gives you the help you
need to live a life which is pleasing to your
heavenly Father.

The Holy Spirit wants to make you into the kind of person that is **loving** and **kind** and **full
of joy**.

Look up and write down these two verses:

GALATIANS 5:22, 23 "THE FRUIT OF THE SPIRIT ?"

_____

_____

_____

Be sure to ask the Holy Spirit
to **grow** this **fruit** in **you**!

Question 60

> **How long ago is it since Christ died?**
> Nearly 2000 years.

This looks like a pretty boring question, doesn't it?
Why is it so important?

When you begin to think about it, it is a very important question. Let me tell you why.

There are many, many GREAT MOMENTS OF HISTORY.

There is the **creation of Adam and Eve!**
There is the **building of the pyramids in Egypt!**
There is the **discovery of America!**
There is the **birth of you!**
These are all **great moments in history.**

But the **most important moment of history**
was when the Lord Jesus died for you!
It really and truly happened! It really and truly happened nearly
2000 years ago!

What the Lord Jesus did 1,900 years ago is a part of history.
It is very important to understand that the story of the Lord Jesus
is not a **make-pretend** story but that it actually happened!

It is also important the know that the Lord Jesus died nearly 2000
years ago because every time you put the DATE on your paper in
school you are telling the teacher and the whole class and anyone
else who reads your paper, that the Lord Jesus died!

Just think! Whenever you put "APRIL 4, 1989"
    (Or whatever date it is!)
you are saying: "The Lord Jesus died for me 1,989 years ago!"

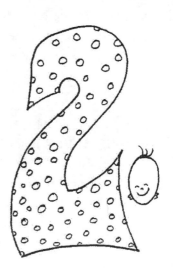

It's funny to realize that even a person who says he is an **atheist**
is saying that the Lord Jesus really did live 1,989 years ago when
he writes the date on his paper!

Question 61

> ### How were pious persons saved before the coming of Christ?
> By believing in a Savior to come.

This is one of the most interesting chapters in the Bible. It contains what someone has called **The Roll Call of The Faithful**. All the men and women mentioned in this chapter lived before the Lord Jesus came. They are all Old Testament men and women.

LISTEN WHILE YOUR TEACHER READS HEBREWS 11:4-32 AND **CIRCLE** THE NAMES OF THESE OLD TESTAMENT MEN AND WOMEN WHO ARE MENTIONED.

Sarah	**Noah**	**Abel**	**Abraham**
Gideon	**Samuel**	**Joseph**	**Moses**
Rahab	**Isaac**	**Jephthah**	**The Prophets**
Samson	**David**	**Enoch**	**Moses' parents**
Adam	**Jacob**		

Is there someone in the lists above that is not mentioned in HEBREWS? Yes, it is _____.

All the people listed in HEBREWS CHAPTER 11 went to heaven because they believed in a Savior who was to come. They lived long before the Lord Jesus, but they believed God's promise to send a Savior. The only difference between the believers in the Old Testament and the believers in the New Testament is this:

   The Old Testament believers believed in a Savior **to come**.

   The New Testament believers believe in a Savior **who came**. Do you see the difference?

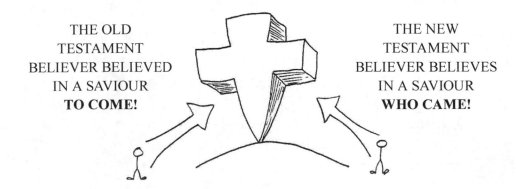

THE OLD TESTAMENT BELIEVER BELIEVED IN A SAVIOUR **TO COME!**

THE NEW TESTAMENT BELIEVER BELIEVES IN A SAVIOUR **WHO CAME!**

Question 62

> <u>**How did they show their faith?**</u>
> By offering sacrifices on God's altar.

One day I asked my dad,

> **"How did the people in the Old Testament know that they were to sacrifice an animal to cover their sins?"**

My dad said,

> **"Because God Taught Adam and Eve That Only Through the Sacrifice Of An Animal Could Their Sins Be Covered. God Gave Them That Lesson In The Garden Of Eden."**

LET'S TURN TO **GENESIS 3:6, 7**. WHAT DID ADAM AND EVE USE TO COVER THEIR NAKEDNESS AFTER THEY SINNED?

I've never worn those things for clothes, and I can imagine that they wouldn't work for school!

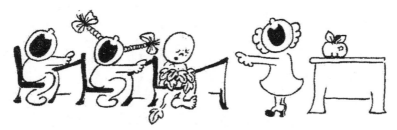

After God spoke to them about their disobedience, He made them some clothes. YOU CAN READ ABOUT IT IN **GENESIS 3:21**.

God took an animal, probably a **lamb**, and killed it. It was the first time in God's beautiful world that anything had died. A **lamb** had to die so that Adam and Eve could be clothed.

Adam and Eve talked about how God had clothed them in the Garden to their children. One of their sons, **Abel**, understood that it was only through the death of a sacrifice that he or anyone else could be accepted by God. READ **GENESIS 4:3-5** AND FIND OUT WHAT ABEL DID.

WHAT DID ABEL BRING TO GOD FOR A SACRIFICE? _____

_____

Was God pleased with it? _____

Catechism for Young Children

Question 63

> **What did these sacrifices represent?**
> Christ, the Lamb of God, who was to die for sinners.

Lambs, lambs, lambs!
Lambs all over the place!

Only God knew that through the years in the Old Testament how many lambs would be sacrificed! Years and years went by. Centuries rolled by and thousands and thousands of lambs were killed!

Through all those years and all those centuries, people knew that the lamb sacrifices could not really take away sins. The lambs pointed to **someone** who would take away sins.

Do you remember the answer to Question 61?
HOW WERE PIOUS PERSONS SAVED BEFORE THE COMING OF CHRIST?

_____

When a person sacrificed a lamb in the Old Testament, he was to look in faith to a time when God would send someone, a Savior, who would take away sin.

And then the time came for that **Someone**, the Savior, to be born!
In what kind of place was the Savior, the Lord Jesus, born?

_____ (**Hint**: it's a part of where lambs live!)

When the Lord Jesus grew up and began His ministry His cousin, John, pointed to Him and said:

(COPY WHAT JOHN SAID IN **JOHN 1:29**)

_____

_____

_____

Question 64

> ## <u>What offices has Christ?</u>
> Christ has three offices.

My grandmother has the neatest office!
She works downtown and lets me go with her sometimes.
Her office is in a high, high building from which I can see almost the whole city.
Grandmother lets me make copies, and answer the phone, and sharpen pencils, and take notes on her notepads.

I like Grandmother's office!

But she also has another office! It's not in a building. Grandmother is on the City Council. Her position on the City Council is Vice-Chairperson. The office of Vice-Chairperson is a very important job.

So I can say that Grandmother has two offices.

One of her offices is in a building. It is a room with a desk, a telephone, and some windows. It is the place where she works.

But her other office is **not** in a building, and it is **not** a room. It is a **position of responsibility**. She is **vice-chairperson**. This second office tells **who** she is and **what** she does.

When we begin to talk about the **offices** of the Lord Jesus, it is important to understand that we are **not** talking about something in a building or a room.

When we talk about the **offices** of the Lord Jesus, we are talking about His **positions of responsibility**.

When the Lord Jesus came, He came to do **special tasks** so that we could one day go to **heaven**. In the next seven Catechism questions we will study these **special tasks**.

Question 65

> **What are they?**
> The offices of a prophet, of a priest, and of a king.

In the **Old Testament,** there were three main offices. Now remember that we said in Question 64, we are **not** talking about buildings but **positions of responsibility**!

In the **Old Testament** there were **Three Main Positions of Responsibility**.

These offices were **Prophet, Priest,** and **King**.

Can you think of anyone in the OLD TESTAMENT   who was a **Prophet**...?
                                                who was a **Priest**...?
                                                who was a **King**...?

First of all, there was a little baby who was hid on the river in a basket. This little baby grew up to be a **Prophet**. (Exodus 2:3)
CAN YOU THINK OF WHO HE WAS?_____

As a **Prophet** this man taught the people about God and how they were to obey God.

Secondly, there was a boy that grew up to be a **Priest**. In fact, he was the first **Priest** in the nation of **Israel**. He was the big brother of **Moses**.
CAN YOU THINK OF WHO HE WAS?_____
You might look it up in EXODUS 4:13, 14.

As a **Priest** this man was to pray for the people and to offer up Sacrifices so that their sins could be forgiven.

And then, last of all, there was a shepherd-boy that God called to be **King** over **Israel**. He was a very great **king**. When he was still a young man, he killed a giant named **Goliath**.

CAN YOU THINK OF WHO HE WAS?_____
As a **king** this man was to rule and guide his people. He was also to lead the army against the nation's enemies.

There were many **Prophets** and **Priests** and **Kings** in the Old Testament. All of them prepared the way for the Lord Jesus. When He came, He was **Prophet, Priest, and King**!

Question 66

> ### How is Christ a prophet?
> Because He teaches us the will of God.

I have the best teacher in school!
I really love being a part of her class!
Now my teacher is not young. I guess she is old enough to be a grandmother, or even older!
My teacher is not beautiful. She has white hair, she wears glasses, and she wears "Old-Lady" shoes!

My teacher is very strict! She expects every student to do the very best they can do.
And she never lets anyone get by with half-done work!

Do you know why I love being in her class? Because she really cares about each one of us!
She helps us when we need help. She encourages us to do our best.
She listens to our problems. And she always tries to help us do the right thing.

One day she told us that she prayed for us... every night!
I never knew teachers did that! But many of them do!

The Lord Jesus was a **teacher**. In the Old Testament they were called **prophets**. The **prophets** in the Old Testament taught people the **will of God**. They taught people about **who God is** and **what god is like** and **what god does**.

When the Lord Jesus was here on earth, He was the **Master Teacher**. Everything He taught was **true** and is **true** today. He never taught any mistakes.

Oh, how people loved to hear Him teach! TURN IN YOUR BIBLE TO MATTHEW 7:28 AND COPY THE VERSE HERE.

_____

_____

_____

_____

The duty of a **Good Teacher** is to point students to the Lord Jesus so that they can obey and do the will of God. You can point others to the Lord Jesus so that they can obey and do the will of God?

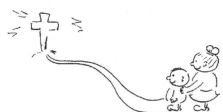

Question 67

> ### How is Christ a priest?
> Because He died for our sins and pleads with God for us.

In the Old Testament, the first person to be a **priest** was the big brother of Moses.
His name was **Aaron**. After Aaron died, only his sons could be priests. There were two main
duties that a priest had.
First, the priest offered **sacrifices** to God for the sins of the people.
PERHAPS IT WOULD BE GOOD TO REVIEW QUESTIONS 61,62, AND 63.

HOW WERE PIOUS PERSONS SAVED BEFORE THE COMING OF CHRIST?
HOW DID THEY SHOW THEIR FAITH?
WHAT DID THESE SACRIFICES REPRESENT?

I hope you remember that the sacrifices did not take away the people's sins.
The sacrifices pointed to **someone** who would take away sins.
That **someone** was the Lord Jesus. He offered up Himself on the cross to die for us.

But there was another important job that the priest did. He prayed for the people.
Have you ever had someone say, "I'm praying for you?" It's so encouraging!
The Lord Jesus prays for each one of us moment by moment.
Isn't that great! He is praying that we will love Him.
He is praying that we will obey Him. He is praying that we will love each other.

HERE ARE TWO VERSES FROM **THE LETTER TO THE HEBREWS**.
SEE IF YOU CAN **MATCH** THE **VERSE** TO THE **DUTIES** OF THE PRIEST.

HEBREWS 7:26 Therefore he is able to save completely those who come to God through him because he always lives to intercede for them.

He died for our sins.

HEBREWS 9:28 Christ was sacrificed once to take away the sins of many people, and he will appear a second time, not to bear sin, but to bring salvation to those who are waiting for him.

He pleads with God for us.

Question 68

<u>**How is Christ a king?**</u>
Because He rules over us and defends us.

Last year, I was elected May King by my class.

Our school celebrates May Day with games and food and fun all day.

At the beginning of the day I was to be crowned as King. Candie Sweetthing was to be crowned Queen.

Candie and I marched down the aisle together to the thrones.

The closer I got to the throne, the I prouder I got.

By the time I got to the throne I was puffed up with pride.

I began to think I was really something great!

Well, the Bible says that God humbles the proud. And He humbled me!

When Candie and I sat down, I missed the throne! I fell off the back of the platform!

Everybody laughed! (Except me!) Some King I turned out to be!

I haven't read about any king who fell off his throne!

Do you remember the Priest had two duties? The King had two very important duties.

First of all, He was the **ruler**. The people were to obey him.

Secondly, He was to **defend** His people. That meant that He was to take care of them and lead them in victory over enemies.

CIRCLE THESE OLD TESTAMENT MEN AND WOMEN WHO ARE LET'S LOOK UP AND COPY TWO VERSES IN SCRIPTURE THAT SHOW HOW THE LORD JESUS **RULES** OVER US AND **DEFENDS** US.

JOHN 15:14_____

_____

EPHESIANS 6:10_____

_____

Question 69

> **Why do you need Christ as a prophet?**
> Because I am ignorant.

"**Ignorant**" does not sound like a very nice word. In fact, a kid at school called me an **ignoramus** once! What do you think an **ignoramus** is?

It sounds like a big green animal with a long snout and four huge eyes! I had to look **ignoramus** up in the dictionary. An **ignoramus** is a person who is **ignorant**.

Then I looked **ignorant** up in the dictionary. **Ignorant** means "knowing little or nothing."

Now the Catechism answer today says that "I am ignorant."

Of what am I ignorant? I do my homework (most of the time!)

Most of all, I am ignorant of God. I do not really know **who** He is, or **what** He is like.

Today we will be studying **PSALM 19**. It is printed below. As you read, you will find out:
1. What we can know about God from **nature**.   2. Why we need the **Bible**.

PSALM 19

1. The heavens declare the glory of God;
    the skies proclaim the work of His hands.

2. Day after day they pour forth speech;
    night after night they display
    knowledge.

3. There is no speech or language where
    their voice is not heard...

7. The **law** of the Lord is perfect,
    reviving the soul.
    The **statutes** of the Lord are trustworthy
    making wise the simple.

8. The **precepts** of the Lord are right,
    giving joy to the heart.
    The **commands** of the Lord are radiant
    giving light to the eyes.

9. The **fear** of the Lord is pure, enduring forever.
    The **ordinances** of the Lord are sure
    and altogether righteous.

10. They are more precious than gold,
    than much pure gold.
    They are sweeter than honey,
    than honey from the comb.

11. By them is your servant warned;
    in keeping them there is great reward.

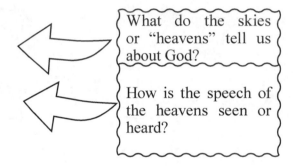

What do the skies or "heavens" tell us about God?

How is the speech of the heavens seen or heard?

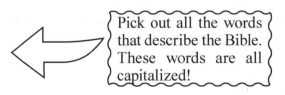

Pick out all the words that describe the Bible. These words are all capitalized!

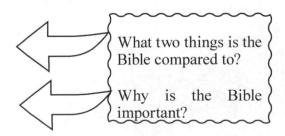

What two things is the Bible compared to?

Why is the Bible important?

Question 70

> ### Why do you need Christ as a priest?
> Because I am guilty.

REVIEW! REVIEW! REVIEW! WHEW! We need to review!
With this Question 70, we need to go back to Questions 28-42.
If we go through those questions, we will understand Question 70.

28. WHAT IS SIN?
29. WHAT IS MEANT BY WANT OF CONFORMITY?
30. WHAT IS MEANT BY TRANSGRESSION?
31. WHAT WAS THE SIN OF OUR FIRST PARENTS?
32. WHO TEMPTED THEM TO THIS SIN?
33. WHAT BEFELL OUR FIRST PARENTS WHEN THEY HAD SINNED?
34. DID ADAM ACT FOR HIMSELF ALONE IN THE COVENANT OF WORKS?
35. WHAT EFFECT HAD THE SIN OF ADAM ON ALL MANKIND?
36. WHAT IS THAT SINFUL NATURE WHICH WE INHERIT FROM ADAM CALLED?
37. WHAT DOES EVERY SIN DESERVE?
38. CAN ANYONE GO TO HEAVEN WITH THIS SINFUL NATURE?
39. WHAT IS A CHANGE OF HEART CALLED?
40. WHO CAN CHANGE A SINNER'S HEART?
41. CAN ANYONE BE SAVED THROUGH THE COVENANT OF WORKS?
42. WHY CAN NONE BE SAVED THROUGH THE COVENANT OF WORKS?

Did you remember all the answers?
Do you know the **six hardest words to say**?
The six hardest words to say are:

Have you ever had to say the six hardest words? We try not to say them.
We say, "It wasn't my fault!" Or we say, "He made me do it!"
It is extremely hard to say: "I WAS WRONG; I AM SORRY."

When we say that we were wrong, then we are saying that we are guilty. We are saying that we are at fault.

Because we are guilty, because we are sinners, the Lord Jesus became our Priest. He was our Sacrifice and died for us.

Question 71

> **<u>Why do you need Christ as a king?</u>**
> Because I am weak and helpless.

When I was younger, I helped my dad mow the yard.
Dad mowed and I picked up sticks and paper.
When I got older, Dad began to let me help with mowing.
And now I mow the yard every Saturday during the summer.
That grass grows so fast! Sometimes I don't feel like mowing the yard, but the grass just keeps growing! One time I didn't mow the yard for two weeks.
Wow! Was the grass ever high! It took a lot longer to mow it the next Saturday!

My Dad said that **sin** is like our grass.
There are **seeds of sin** in my life that pop up all over the place.
When I want to be good, often times I'm bad.
When I plan to say good things, often times I say things which are not good at all!
I need **someone** to help me be the kind of person God wants me to be.
And that **someone** is the **Lord Jesus**.
He is my **King**. When I call Him **Lord**, I am calling Him **King**.
He is not only my **Savior**, but He is my **Lord** as well.

FILL IN THE BLANKS
Put the OFFICE of Christ with the RIGHT DEFINITION.

1. As our _____, Jesus DIED for us.

2. As our _____, Jesus DEFENDS us.

3. As our _____, Jesus TEACHES us.

4. As our _____, Jesus RULES over us.

Question 72

> **How many commandments did God give on Mount Sinai?**
> Ten Commandments.

Are you ready to move forward?
So far you have memorized 71 Catechism answers!
Remember: **review! review! review!**
Reviewing what we have learned helps us not to forget!

These lessons to come will be the **best** yet in Catechism
As you **keep up**, you won't **fall behind**.

Here we go for more important lessons! We are going to learn about:

The Ten Commandments,
The Lord's Prayer,
Baptism,
The Lord's Supper,
and **The Lord's Second Coming!**

I have told you the **five** things which we will be studying.
Now I want you to MATCH these FIVE things with FIVE SCRIPTURE PASSAGES!
SCRIPTURE PASSAGES and DRAW A LINE to SUBJECT:

The Ten Commandments	I Thessalonians 4:16-18
The Lord's Prayer	I Corinthians 11:23-26
Baptism	Exodus 20:1-17
The Lord's Supper	Matthew 6:9-13
The Second Coming	Acts 16:29-34

Question 73

<u>What Are the Ten Commandments called</u>?
The Decalogue.

As a third grader, you are smarter than you were in first grade. I certainly hope you are!

Kitty and I are now in third grade.
We are learning so many new things.

We are learning to write in **cursive**.
We are learning our multiplication tables (Oh boy!).
We are learning to spell longer and harder words.

I guess you know by now that in Catechism we are learning many new words.
Can you remember the meaning of these words?

Regeneration   **Sanctification**
Atonement   **Repentance**
Justification

You haven't forgotten them, have you?

The new word today is "**decalogue**."
It is a combination of two Greek words:

Deca = "ten"   Logos = "words"

The Ten Commandments were first called "The Ten Words."

LOOK UP **EXODUS 20:1-17**.

WHO GAVE THE TEN COMMANDMENTS? (Think hard!)

CAN YOU FIND THE FIRST FOUR COMMANDMENTS? VERSES 3- _____

CAN YOU FIND THE LAST SIX COMMANDMENTS? VERSES 12- _____

WHO DID GOD USE TO GIVE US THE TEN COMMANDMENTS? _____
(It doesn't tell us, but you can guess!)

Catechism for Young Children

Question 74

> ## What do the first four commandments teach?
> Our duty to God.

Kitty and I have been brother and sister since she was born.
Kitty is younger than I because I was born before her.
So that makes me her BIG BROTHER!

We get along most of the time.
We really love each other, and we want to do good things for each other.

I want to do the "right" thing for her.
And she wants to do the "right" thing for me.
It is our "duty" to do right.
It is our duty because we love each other.

It is our "duty" to obey God because we love Him.
We love Him because He first loved us.
IF YOU READ **EXODUS 20:1, 2**, YOU WILL SEE HOW MUCH GOD LOVED HIS
PEOPLE, THE ISRAELITES.

I am the Lord your God who brought you out of _____."
Because God loves us so much, then we love Him.
And when we love God, we want to obey Him.
It is our duty.

NOW TURN BACK TO **EXODUS 20. LOOK AT VERSES 3-11.**
PUT THE FIRST FOUR COMMANDMENTS IN ORDER.
WRITE THE NUMBER (1, 2, 3, OR 4) IN THE BLANKS.

YOU SHALL NOT MISUSE THE NAME OF THE LORD YOUR GOD.
REMEMBER THE SABBATH DAY BY KEEPING IT HOLY.
YOU SHALL HAVE NO OTHER GODS BEFORE ME.
YOU SHALL NOT MAKE FOR YOURSELF AN IDOL.

WRITE OUT JOHN 14:15 _____

_____

_____

Question 75

> **What do the last six commandments teach?**
> Our duty to our fellow men.

IV said that I could teach the lesson today. (Thank you, big brother!)
We are going to look at the last six commandments.
The last six commandments teach about **relationships**.

The **most important relationship** of all is our relationship with our heavenly Father.
Are you a member of God's Forever Family?

The other relationships are
> **Our family**
> **Our church**
> **Our school**
> **Our neighbors.**

Our heavenly Father is very interested in people. He loves all people. He sent His Son to live and to die for us so that we might be with Him. There are going to be many people in heaven.

We are to live in such a way that other people will want to know and trust our heavenly Father.

MY RELATIONSHIP TO MY HEAVENLY FATHER

MY RELATIONSHIP TO OTHERS

TURN ONCE AGAIN TO EXODUS 20:12-17. PUT THE LAST SIX COMMANDMENTS IN ORDER. WRITE THE NUMBER (5, 6, 7, 8, 9, 10, 11, 12) IN THE BLANKS.

YOU SHALL NOT STEAL   _____

HONOR YOUR FATHER AND YOUR MOTHER   _____

YOU SHALL NOT COVET   _____

YOU SHALL NOT COMMIT ADULTERY   _____

YOU SHALL NOT GIVE FALSE TESTIMONY   _____

YOU SHALL NOT MURDER   _____

Catechism for Young Children

Question 76

What is the sum of the Ten Commandments? To love God with all my heart, and my neighbor as myself.

Today we are going to make valentines!
Well, not really valentines, but we are going to draw **hearts**.
I know that you can draw hearts.

♡   ♡   ♡   ♡   ♡   ♡   ♡   ♡

In my **quiet time** this morning, I read from **I JOHN, chapter 4**.
I was amazed how many times the word **love** appears there.
Below is the passage I read.
I want you to draw a heart around each word **"love."**
After you have made all your hearts, fill in these blanks:

"WHOEVER LOVES _____ MUST ALSO LOVE HIS _____."

♡ "DEAR FRIENDS, LET US **LOVE** ONE ANOTHER, FOR **LOVE** COMES FROM GOD. EVERYONE WHO **LOVES** HAS BEEN BORN OF GOD AND KNOWS GOD. WHOEVER DOES NOT **LOVE** DOES NOT KNOW GOD, BECAUSE GOD IS **LOVE**.

♡ THIS IS HOW GOD SHOWED HIS **LOVE** AMONG US: HE SENT HIS ONE AND ONLY SON INTO THE WORLD THAT WE MIGHT LIVE THROUGH HIM.

♡ THIS IS **LOVE**: NOT THAT WE **LOVED** GOD, BUT THAT HE **LOVED** US AND SENT HIS SON AS AN ATONING SCRIPTURE FOR OUR SINS.

♡ WE **LOVE** BECAUSE HE FIRST **LOVED** US. IF ANYONE SAY, 'I **LOVE** GOD,' YET HATES HIS BROTHER, HE IS A LIAR.

♡ WHOEVER **LOVES** GOD MUST ALSO **LOVE** HIS BROTHER."

By the way, what is **"an atoning sacrifice for our sins?"**
The answer is found in Catechism Question 48:

WHAT IS MEANT BY THE ATONEMENT? _____ (Can you repeat the answer?)

Question 77

> ### Who is your neighbor?
> All my fellow men are my neighbors.

Today we are going to do some **inductive bible study**.
I hope that **inductive bible study** does not sound hard.
In fact, you have already done some of it!
Turn back to Question 69 and see what you did!

Below is a story in LUKE 10 which Jesus told.
See if you can answer the questions in the right column together.

LUKE 10:30-36

30.	"A man was going down from Jerusalem to Jericho, when he fell into the hands of robbers. They stripped him of his clothes, beat him and went away, leaving him half dead.	WHO are the four men of this story?
31.	A priest happened to be going down the same road, and when he saw the man, he passed by on the other side.	WHAT did the priest, the Levite and the Samaritan do to help the man?
32.	So too, a Levite, when he came to the place and saw him, passed by on the other side.	
33.	But a Samaritan, as he traveled, came where the man was, and when he saw him, he took pity on him.	WHY did the Samaritan help the man?
34.	He went to him and bandaged his wounds, pouring on oil and wine. Then he put the man on his own donkey, took him to an inn and took care of him.	
35.	The next day he took out two denarii and gave them to the innkeeper. 'Look after him,' he said, 'and when I return, I will reimburse you for any extra expense you may have.'	HOW did he help the man?
36.	Which of these three do you think was a neighbor to the man who fell into the hands of robbers?"	WHEN are **you** to help others?

LOOK IT UP! WHO WAS THE HURT MAN'S NEIGHBOR? **LUKE 10:36**

WHO IS YOUR NEIGHBOR? _____ my fellow men are my neighbors.

Questions 78 and 79

> **Is God pleased with those who love and obey him?**
> Yes, He says, "I love them that love me."
>
> **Is God displeased with those who do not love and obey him?**
> Yes; "God is angry with the wicked every day."

Where do those two verses come from?
LOOK UP THESE TWO VERSES AND MATCH THEM!

PSALM 7:11   "I love them that love me."

PROVERBS 8:17   "God is angry with the wicked every day."

The Bible is full of real people who walked with and loved God!
There is a chapter in the New Testament about some of these people.

TURN IN YOUR BIBLE to **HEBREWS 11**.

Each verse tells of a man or a woman who loved God. Because they loved God, they pleased God.
Write the NAME of the person next to the verse.

VERSE 4 _____   VERSE 5 _____

VERSE 7 _____   VERSE 8 _____

VERSE 20 _____   VERSE 21 _____

VERSE 22 _____   VERSE 23 _____

VERSE 24 _____   VERSE 31 _____

Now, look back over those same verses.
There are TWO WORDS which are next to every name you have written.
What are those TWO WORDS?
Write those TWO WORDS: _B_____   F_____

According to verse 6, what pleases God? _____
_____

Questions 80 and 81

> **Which is the first commandment?**
> The first commandment is:
> "Thou shalt have no other gods before me."
>
> **What does the first commandment teach us?**
> To worship God alone.

The Bible tells us of a boy named Samuel who lived with a priest named Eli.
Now Eli was a very kind priest, but he was not a good father. Eli had two sons who were wicked.

Poor Eli! He did not ever discipline his sons!
The Bible says that Eli loved his sons more than he loved God!

Eli's sons hated God, and Eli loved his sons more than he loved God.
Now Samuel lived with Eli and his sons, but Samuel loved God more than anything else.

One night God spoke to Samuel! Samuel had never heard God speak.
And he didn't know what God's voice sounded like. Samuel had already gone to bed and was fast asleep when God woke him up.

TURN IN YOUR BIBLE to **I SAMUEL 3 and read the first 10 verses**. It is a wonderful story.

How many times did God wake Samuel? _____ Whom did Samuel think had called him? _____
Write out Samuel's answer to God after God called him three times.

_____

_____

A **servant** is a person that serves a **master**.
Samuel said that he was God's **servant**.
The Lord God was Samuel's **master**.

Samuel, even as a young boy, worshipped God alone.
Samuel had no other gods before him.

Samuel!
Samuel!

Catechism for Young Children

Questions 82 and 83

<u>**Which is the second commandment?**</u>
The second commandment is:
"Thou shalt not make unto thee any graven image,
or any likeness of anything that is in heaven above,
or that is in the earth beneath,
or that is in the water under the earth:
thou shalt not bow down thyself to them, nor serve them:
for I, the Lord thy God, am a jealous God,
visiting the iniquity of the fathers upon the children
unto the third and fourth generation of them that hate me,
and showing mercy unto thousands of them that love me,
and keep my commandments."

<u>**What does the second commandment teach us?**</u>
To worship God in a proper manner,
and to avoid idolatry.

Today you will need your Bible.
In the **Old Testament** and the **New Testament** many people worshipped false gods.
They made idols to represent these false gods. Wherever the Gospel was believed, men and women turned from their false idols to worship and serve the living God.

We are never, never, to allow anything in our lives to be more important than the Lord Jesus.
We are to offer all that we are and have to the Lord Jesus for Him to control and use.

TURN IN YOUR BIBLE to **ACTS 19:17-20**. This is about the Church in the city of Ephesus.
Before they became Christians, many of the people worshipped and served false gods.
But when they became Christians, oh, what a difference!

In **ACTS 19:18**, what is the first thing the people did after they believed in the Lord Jesus?

_____

_____

COPY **ACTS 19:20**_____

_____

_____

Questions 84 and 85

<u>Which is the third commandment?</u>
The third commandment is:
"Thou shalt not take the name of
the Lord thy God in vain,
for the Lord will not hold him guiltless
that taketh His name in vain."

<u>What does the third commandment teach us?</u>
To reverence God's Name, Word, and works.

Our Youth Director taught our youth group how to canoe today! I thought it was going to be easy. Was I wrong! There Are important of things to learn about canoeing: 1. How to get in/out of the canoe. 2. How to paddle forward/backwards. 3. How to change positions with your partner!

After canoeing we made a campfire and our Youth Director talked with us. He talked about **God's name, God's word, and God's works.**

He told us about God's beautiful world. God made it, and He wants us to take care of it. He also made our bodies. We are to take care of them, too. The Bible says, **"I am fearfully and wonderfully made."**

Our Youth Director then talked about God's wonderful Word. We are to read God's Word and obey it. God's Word is to be our spiritual food. When we obey God's Word we are kept from sinning against God. The Bible says, **"I have hidden your word in my heart."**

And then our Youth Director told us something very sad. He said that during the day some of us had used God's Name in vain. We were all surprised and wondered who had done that. He said that most of us had. Whenever we had said, **"O God!"** when we were playing with each other, we were taking God's Name in vain, because we were not speaking with Him.

We must never use God's Name lightly.

MATCH THE VERSE WITH THE REFERENCE:

"I am fearfully and wonderfully made."	**PSALM 8:1**
"I have hidden your Word in my heart that I might not sin."	**PSALM 119:11**
"Lord, our Lord, how majestic is your name in all the earth!"	**PSALM 139:14**

Question 86

> **Which is the fourth commandment?**
> The fourth commandment is:
> "Remember the Sabbath day, to keep it holy.
> Six days shalt thou labor, and do all thy work:
> but the seventh day is the Sabbath of the Lord thy God:
> in it thou shalt not do any work,
> thou, nor thy son, nor thy daughter,
> thy manservant, nor thy maidservant, nor thy cattle,
> nor thy stranger that is within thy gates:
> for in six days the Lord made heaven and earth,
> the sea, and all that in them is,
> and rested the seventh day:
> wherefore the Lord blessed the Sabbath day,
> and hallowed it."

This is a new word for us: **Sabbath**. It is a Hebrew word which means "**rest**."

OPEN YOUR BIBLE TO GENESIS 2:1-3. What did God do on the seventh day of creation?

_____

In the **Old Testament** the **Sabbath** was on the last day of the week.

What day was that?_____

In the **New Testament** the **Sabbath** is on the first day of the week.

What day was that?_____

The Day of Rest is to be a very special day for believers.
What are some of the special things we do on the **Sabbath** day?

1._____

2._____

3. _____

In this commandment, God tells us that we are **not** to _____ on the **Sabbath** day.

In this commandment, God tells us that we are to _____ The Lord _____
the Sabbath day, and _____ it. "Hallowed" meant He kept it holy.

Question 87

What does the fourth commandment teach us?
To keep the Sabbath holy.

What does **"holy"** mean?
I bet that you've got some ideas about it!
Below is the definition of "**holy**."
The letters are scrambled, so see if you can figure them out!

ETS TAARP

Holy means

"_____"

Something that is **holy** is something that is **set apart** for very special use.
God's Name is **holy**. That is why we are to reverence His Name. We are not to use **God's Name** as a joke or as a curse.

God's Sabbath is **holy** also. It is a very special day. It is to be used in a very special way.

TURN TO **GENESIS 2:2, 3**.

What did God do after He finished creating the world and all that was in it?

_____

In **GENESIS 2:3** what are the two things God did to the seventh day?

1._____   2._____

The **Sabbath** is to be a of **day rest**. God blesses the **Sabbath** and makes it holy.

Because it is a **day** of **rest**, we are not to do our normal work on that day. Sometimes it is easy to wait until Sunday afternoon to do our homework for school the next day. But schoolwork is our normal work. We need to do it before Sunday!

The **Sabbath** also is a **day** of **joy**. We go to worship with other Christians. It should give us great **happiness** to come together with others to study God's Word and to pray.

Is the **Sabbath** a special day for you? Is it a day of **rest** and **joy**?

Questions 88 and 89

> **What day of the week is the Christian Sabbath?**
> The first day of the week, called the Lord's Day.
>
> **Why is it called the Lord's Day?**
> Because on that day Christ rose from the dead.

Our Lord Jesus rose from the dead on Sunday morning.
Every Sunday morning when we go to Church, we celebrate His resurrection from the dead.
Every Sunday morning, we celebrate Easter.

Now 2,000 years ago the early Christians did not call this day of the week "**Sunday**." In **The New Testament** there are three names for this day.
LOOK UP THESE VERSES AND THEN WRITE OUT WHAT THIS DAY WAS CALLED IN THE **NEW TESTAMENT**.

MARK 16:2 "_____ day of the _____ "
ACTS 2:1 "Day of _____ "
REVELATION 1:10 "_____ _____ day"

Here is a song to learn:

"O day of rest and gladness, O day of joy and light,
O balm of care and sadness, Most beautiful, most bright;
On thee the high and lowly, through ages joined in tune,
Sing 'HOLY, HOLY, HOLY,' To the great God Triune.

"On thee, at the creation, the light first had its birth;
On thee, for our salvation, Christ rose from depths of earth;
On thee our Lord victorious The Spirit sent from heaven.
And thus on thee most glorious A triple light was given."

Catechism for Young Children

Question 90

How should the Sabbath be spent?
In prayer and praise,
in hearing and reading God's Word,
and in doing good to our fellow men.

On the Sabbath we usually go to Church to worship together.
Because we are celebrating Jesus' resurrection, it is a day of joy and excitement.

We come together to offer prayer and praise to our heavenly Father.
We come together to hear and read God's Word. In Sunday School, we study God's Word together. We come together to help each other. Sometimes we learn that others in our world have very special needs. That is why we give our tithes and offerings-- to help others in need.

On the Sabbath we do not only go to Church.
We are also to be very aware of helping others around us.
Perhaps there are some in our neighborhood who do not go to Church. Have you invited them?
Perhaps there are some in our neighborhood who are shut ins.
The Lord's Day could be used to spend some time with these shut ins.
Perhaps even our mothers could use some time off from the kitchen. Maybe you can offer to set the table and wash the dishes afterwards without being asked.
Perhaps there is a Nursing Home close by, and you and your youth group could plan a Sunday afternoon to visit the men and women there.
This would also be a good day for a nap. Maybe you need to catch up on your sleep!

LOOK UP **I CORINTHIANS 16:1-3**.

WHAT WAS TO BE COLLECTED ON THE LORD'S DAY?

_____

WHAT WAS IT TO BE USED FOR?

_____

LOOK UP **MALACHI 3:10, 11** AND COMPLETE THESE VERSES:

"BRING THE WHOLE _____ INTO THE STOREHOUSE,... AND SEE IF ILL NOT THROW OPEN THE FLOODGATES OF _____ AND POUR OUT SO MUCH _____ THAT YOU WILL NOT HAVE ROOM ENOUGH FOR IT!"

Questions 91 and 92

> **Which is the fifth commandment?**
> The fifth commandment is,
> "Honor thy father and thy mother:
> that thy days may be long upon the land
> which the Lord thy God giveth thee."
>
> **What does the fifth commandment teach us?**
> To love and obey our parents and teachers.

THERE ARE THREE VERY IMPORTANT PLACES WHICH GOD HAS GIVEN YOU WHERE YOU CAN LEARN TO LOVE AND OBEY YOUR PARENTS AND TEACHERS. CAN YOU NAME THESE THREE PLACES?

1. _____

2. _____

3. _____

THINK AND TALK ABOUT: Who are the people in these three places that you are to love and obey?

TURN IN YOUR BIBLE TO LUKE 2:41-52. In verse 51 when the Lord Jesus went home to Nazareth, what kind of son was He to Mary and Joseph?

O _ _ _ _ _ _ _

When the Lord Jesus was obedient to Mary and Joseph, God's Word tells us what kind of Person he became.

COPY VERSE 52 which tells us what kind of Person He became. _____

_____

_____

Questions 93 and 94

Which is the sixth commandment?
The sixth commandment is,
"Thou shalt not kill."

What does the sixth commandment teach us?
To avoid angry passions.

When this commandment tells us not to "kill," it means that we are not to "murder."
We must kill plants and animals to eat. We are not to murder other people.

TURN IN YOUR BIBLE TO **GENESIS 4:1-8**.

Name the four people in this passage.

1. _____   2. _____

3. _____   4. _____

Cain and Abel were brothers, sons of Adam and Eve. Cain and Abel brought offerings to the Lord.

Cain brought_____

Abel brought_____

Which brother was God pleased with? _____

How did Cain feel about this? _____

An angry passion is a very bad feeling of hate for another person.
When we do not avoid angry passions, sometimes we do bad things.

What did Cain's angry passions cause him to do to Abel?

_____

TURN IN YOUR BIBLE TO **I JOHN 3:11-15**. This is <u>not</u> John's Gospel!

In verse 11, what are we to give to others? _____

Verse 15 says that if we hate others, we do **not** have what?

It is so important to **love** and not to hate.
It is important to **control** any angry passions we have.
It is important to **avoid** angry passions!

Questions 95 and 96

> **<u>Which is the seventh commandment?</u>**
> The seventh commandment is,
> "Thou shalt not commit adultery."
>
> **<u>What does the seventh commandment teach us?</u>**
> To be pure in heart, language, and conduct.

The meaning of the word "**adultery**" is **unfaithful**. When you are brought into God's Forever Family, you must choose each day to be **faithful** to God or **unfaithful** to God.

To be **faithful** to God is to love and obey Him.
To be **unfaithful** to God is to choose to disobey Him.

To the child of God, it ought to be easy to be **faithful** to God!
We ought to **always** choose to be **faithful** to our heavenly Father!
But we don't always make that choice, do we?

Often, we choose to be very **unfaithful** to our heavenly **Father!**
We choose to watch TV programs that are not good for us.
We choose to read comic books that are not pure.
We choose to sing popular songs that are not clean.

Whenever we choose to be **unfaithful** to God, we commit **ADULTERY**.
Some people commit adultery with their bodies.
Some people commit adultery with their ears and eyes.
Some people commit adultery with their minds.

The Lord Jesus tells us how to be faithful to God in the Bible.

TURN IN YOUR BIBLE to **LUKE 10:27** and fill in the missing words:

"_____ the lord your God with all your _____ and with all your _____ and with all your _____ and with all your _____: and _____ your _____ as _____."

Catechism for Young Children

Questions 97 and 98

<u>Which is the eighth commandment?</u>
The eighth commandment is,
"Thou shalt not steal."

<u>What does the eighth commandment teach us?</u>
To be honest and industrious.

Do you have some jobs to do around your home? I do. I take out the trash. I rake the yard.
Kitty also has some jobs. She sets the table for meals. She sweeps the walkway.
We take turns feeding Saltine!

My mom and dad are teaching us how to work! Sometimes it's not much fun!
I would rather be doing other things...Like watching TV, or playing Soccer, or riding my bike.

Mom and dad say that it is so important to learn to work.
It is important to learn to enjoy work.
My dad goes to work every morning.
My mom teaches fourth graders and works in the home.

They have told Kitty and me that work is a **joy**.
They have told us that God has given us strong bodies and healthy minds to use for His glory.
One way we glorify God is to do our work cheerfully and well.

The Bible talks about work being good for us.
TURN IN YOUR BIBLE to **GENESIS 2:15** AND WRITE IT DOWN.

_____

_____

_____

And the Bible also talks about **being lazy**!
TURN IN YOUR BIBLE TO **II THESSALONIANS 3:10**.
Fill in these blanks from that verse:

"IF A MAN WILL NOT _____, HE SHALL NOT _____."
God gives us two very wonderful activities: work and play.
We need to learn how to do both!

Questions 99 and 100

> **Which is the ninth commandment?**
> The ninth commandment is,
> "Thou shalt not bear false witness
> against thy neighbor."
>
> **What does the ninth commandment teach us?**
> To tell the truth.

Of the last six commandments, this one is probably the easiest to break!
Look up each of these words: "**bear**" and "**false**" and "**witness**"

BEAR (not the fuzzy animal) _____

FALSE _____

WITNESS _____

Now, put all these definitions together and what do they mean?

_____

What if you hear something that is **True**, but **Bad** about someone?
Can you tell that to others? READ **EPHESIANS 4:29**. Copy this verse below.

"DO NOT LET ANY UNWHOLESOME TALK COME OUT OF YOUR MOUTHS, BUT
ONLY WHAT IS _____

_____

_____

_____

DISCUSS IN CLASS:

1. What is **unwholesome talk**?
2. How do we **build others up** with our words?

Questions 101 and 102

> ## Which is the tenth commandment?
> The tenth commandment is,
> "Thou shalt not covet thy neighbor's house,
> thou shalt not covet thy neighbor's wife,
> nor his manservant, nor his maidservant,
> nor his ox, nor his ass,
> nor anything that is thy neighbor's."
>
> ## What does the tenth commandment teach us?
> To be content with our lot.

There are two important words in the box above which begin with the letter "C."
They are "**covet**" and "**content**."

To **covet** what someone else has is to **long for** what they have.
To **covet** means that I am **jealous** of someone else, I am not **content** with what I have.

To be **content** is to be **satisfied** with what I have.
To be **content** means that I am **grateful** to God for what I have.
To be **content** means that I am **happy** when others are blessed.

Below are the two words: **covet** and **content**.

See if you can look at the 12 words below the spaces
and match them to the correct letter.
The words will tell you more about what **covet** and **content** mean!

C _____   C _____

O _____   O _____

V _____   T _____

E _____   E _____

T _____   N _____

Contentious	Teachable	Envy	Ornery	Nice	Thankful
Enjoyment	Open-Hearted	Noble	Vengeful	Take	Calm

DISCUSS IN CLASS: How do each of these words tell you something about the words, COVET or CONTENT?

Questions 103 and 104

<u>Can any man keep these ten commandments perfectly?</u>
No mere man, since the fall of Adam, ever did or can keep
the Ten Commandments perfectly.

<u>Of what use are the Ten Commandments to us?</u>
They teach us our duty and show our need of a Savior.

Only One Person has ever completely **obeyed** God, or totally **pleased** God! Only One Person
has ever been **perfect**!

His Name is _____!

That's right. I love God and want to obey Him. I don't obey Him all the time.
Because I fall short of loving and obeying God, He sent the Lord Jesus to live and die for me. When
I trust the Lord Jesus for my salvation, He forgives me my sins and makes me ready for heaven!

But that's not all! Until I go to heaven, I am to live my life for the Lord Jesus. I am to seek to
please Him. I am to serve others.

Today I want you to review some Catechism questions.
These are questions you have had during this study. Let's see if you remember them!

23. WHAT COVENANT DID GOD MAKE WITH ADAM?
24. WHAT WAS ADAM BOUND TO DO BY THE COVENANT OF WORKS?
27. DID ADAM KEEP THE COVENANT OF WORKS?
34. DID ADAM ACT FOR HIMSELF ALONE IN THE COVENANT OF WORKS?
35. WHAT EFFECT HAD THE SIN OF ADAM ON ALL MANKIND?
37. WHAT DOES EVERY SIN DESERVE?
38. CAN ANYONE GO TO HEAVEN WITH THIS SINFUL NATURE?
42. WHY CAN NONE BE SAVED THROUGH THE COVENANT OF WORKS?
50. WHAT IS JUSTIFICATION?
51. WHAT IS SANCTIFICATION?
55. WHO WILL BE SAVED?
56. WHAT IS IT TO REPENT?
57. WHAT IS IT TO BELIEVE OR HAVE FAITH IN CHRIST?
67. HOW IS CHRIST A PRIEST?
70. WHY DO YOU NEED CHRIST AS A PRIEST?

Whew! That's enough of a review for today! I hope you have remembered them all. But then
that is what a review is for!

Question 105

<u>What is prayer?</u>
Prayer is asking God for things which He has promised to give.

Prayer is the greatest thing you can ever do for someone else!
When we pray, we ask God for things He has promised to give.

It is important to understand that our heavenly Father has **not** promised to give us everything that we **want**.
It is important to understand that our heavenly Father has **not** promised to give us everything that we **wish**.

You are probably like me. I **want** a lot of things.
I **want** a new **football**.
I **want** a new **bike**.
I **want** a new **fishing rod**. I **wish** I had all these things and **more**!
I **want**, I **want**, I **want**! God has not promised to give me everything I want.

God has promised to give me things that are so much greater than a **football**,
or a **bike**, or a **fishing rod**.

Some of the wonderful things God has promised to give us are found in these verses:

TURN IN YOUR BIBLE to **JOHN 6:47**. God has promised you _____

LUKE 11:13. God has promised you _____

ACTS 1:8. God has promised you _____

EPHESIANS 2:10. God has promised you _____

I JOHN 1:7. God has promised you _____

There are thousands of other things God has promised you.
You will find them in God's Word and claim them by **prayer**!

Question 106

In whose name should we pray?
Only in the name of Christ.

IV and I worked for Ben Weatherstaff today.
He is the gardener at Misselthwaite Manor.
Misselthwaite Manor is a big, big house out in the country.
Ben Weatherstaff asked us if we would like to help him rake leaves.
He said that he would pay us if we did good work.

At the end of the day we were so tired. We had worked very hard.
Ben Weatherstaff thought we had worked hard, too. He paid each of us five dollars!
He paid us by check. This is what it looked like:

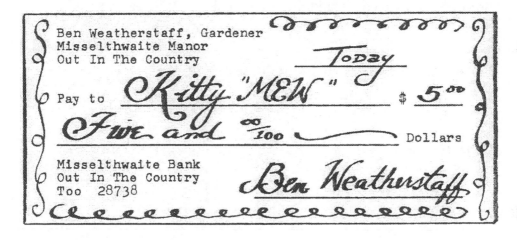

This was the first check IV or I had ever received! Daddy said the bank would cash it for us.
Ben Weatherstaff's signature meant that there was five dollars in the bank for me!
The reason I knew the five dollars was for me was that my name is on the check!
Can you find and circle my name?

When I come in prayer to my heavenly Father, it is like this check. My heavenly Father is so, so very rich. I ask Him every day to take care of me. And He does!
Do you know why? It is because of what the Lord Jesus has done for me.
I can ask my heavenly Father for the things He has promised to give because the Lord Jesus died for me. Jesus' Name is on my "heavenly check!"

Questions 107, 108, and 109

<u>What has Christ given us to teach us how to pray?</u>
The Lord's Prayer.

<u>Repeat the Lord's Prayer</u>

"Our Father which art in heaven,
Hallowed be thy Name.
Thy kingdom come.
Thy will be done in earth, as it is in heaven.
Give us this day our daily bread.
And forgive us our debts, as we forgive our debtors.
and lead us not into temptation, but deliver us from evil:
For thine is the kingdom, and the power, and the glory, forever.
Amen."

<u>How many petitions are there in the Lord's Prayer?</u>
Six

When I was a little boy, I learned a prayer. It started like this: "Now I lay me down to sleep..."
Did you ever learn that prayer?

All of us know **how** to pray. However, all of us do not know **what** to pray.
Jesus taught us **how** to pray. Jesus also taught us **what** to pray.

Perhaps in your Church on Sundays, the people use this prayer:
We call it "**the Lord's Prayer**." It is called that because the Lord Jesus taught it to us.

There are **six petitions** in the Lord's Prayer. LOOK UP "**petition**" in a dictionary.

PETITION _____

_____

_____

TO WHOM are we speaking in the Lord's Prayer?

_____

WHERE does the Lord's Prayer tell us "Our Father" <u>is</u>?

_____

Questions 110 and 111

> **What is the first petition?**
> "Hallowed be thy name."
>
> **What do we pray for in the first petition?**
> That God's name may be honored by us and all men.

Here is another new word: "**hallowed**"
Let's get out the old' dictionary again on this word!

HALLOWED: _____

_____

_____

_____

_____

Do you remember that we have talked about God's Name before?
Do you remember when?
Right! It was when we discussed the Ten Commandments!
So let's REVIEW!

| 84. | WHICH IS THE THIRD COMMANDMENT? |
| 85. | WHAT DOES THE THIRD COMMANDMENT TEACH US? |

God is **holy**.
We do not make Him holy.
But we are to keep His Name holy.
We are not to use His Name in jokes.
We are not to use His Name loosely.

TURN IN YOUR BIBLE to **PSALM 145:1, 2**. COPY THESE VERSES BELOW.
PSALM 145:1, 2

_____

_____

_____

Questions 112 and 113

> **What is the second petition?**
> "Thy kingdom come."
>
> **What do we pray for in the second petition?**
> That the gospel may be preached in all the world and believed and obeyed by us and all men.

Today we are going to MATCH verses with references.
After you have matched, you will know more about God's Kingdom!
Before you match these verses below, you might want to have a SWORD DRILL in class.
Your teacher can be the SWORD DRILL INSTRUCTOR. Use the references below.

_____   Those trusting their riches cannot enter God's kingdom.

_____   God's kingdom belongs to the poor in spirit.

_____   You must be born again to enter God's kingdom.

_____   Only those who do God's will shall be allowed to come into God's kingdom.

_____   The person who lives in God's kingdom will live a life of righteousness, peace, and joy in the holy spirit.

                            We are to seek God's kingdom and his righteousness first.

MATTHEW 7:21
ROMANS 14:17
MATTHEW 5:3
MATTHEW 6:33
JOHN 3:3
LUKE 18:24

Questions 114 and 115

What is the third petition?
"Thy will be done in earth, as it is in heaven."

What do we pray for in the third petition?
That man on earth may serve God
as the angels do in Heaven.

Heaven is a wonderful place!
If you are trusting Christ alone for salvation,
then that is where you are going!
God has created **special beings** who live in Heaven.
These **special beings** sometimes watch over us.
Sometimes they help us.

These **special beings** are **angels**.
Angels always do the will of God.
They are called in the Bible, **Holy Angels**.
When **God** sends them to do a thing, they
perfectly obey.

Many years ago God sent an Angel to do
something very important.
He was to announce the birth of the Lord Jesus!

TURN IN YOUR BIBLE to **LUKE 1:26-38**.
WHAT WAS THE ANGEL'S NAME?

_____

WHAT WAS THE NAME OF JESUS'
MOTHER?

_____

Questions 116 and 117

What is the fourth petition?
"Give us this day our daily bread."

What do we pray for in the fourth petition?
That God would give us all things needful for our bodies and souls.

There was once a very great prophet in Israel.
His name was **Elijah**.
While Elijah was a prophet, a very wicked king ruled Israel.
His name was **Ahab**.
Ahab wanted to kill Elijah.
But God hid Elijah and took care of him.

TURN IN YOUR BIBLE to **I KINGS 17:1-16**.
These verses tell how God took care of Elijah.

WHAT DID GOD ORDER TO FEED ELIJAH IN VERSE 4? _____
WHAT DID GOD GIVE HIM TO DRINK IN VERSE 4?
_____

WHOM DID GOD USE TO FEED ELIJAH IN VERSE 9?
_____

See if you can tell in your own words the story of the Widow at Zarephath.

TURN IN YOUR BIBLE to **MATTHEW 6:25-33**.

WHAT ANIMAL DOES VERSE 26
SAY GOD TAKES CARE OF?   _____

WHAT PLANT DOES GOD CARE
FOR IN VERSE 28?   _____

FILL IN THE BLANKS:

MATTHEW 6:33 "BUT **S**_____ **F**_____ GOD'S KINGDOM AND HIS **R**_____,
AND **A**_____ THESE THINGS WILL BE GIVEN TO YOU AS WELL."

Catechism for Young Children

Questions 118 and 119

What is the fifth petition?
"And forgive us our debts, as we forgive our debtors."

What do we pray for in the fifth petition?
That God would pardon our sins for Christ's sake,
and enable us to forgive those who have injured us.

A long time ago there lived a lady named Corrie ten Boom.
She lived in Holland with her father and her sister.
The three of them lived a very quiet, happy life together.

One day a group of soldiers came into their town.
The soldiers put many, many people into prison.
Corrie and her father and sister were put into prison.

The reason that Corrie and her father and sister were put into prison was because they were
Christians. Because they were Christians, they had been trying to help others.
The soldiers did not like that and put them into prison.

Corrie's father died in prison.
And Corrie's sister died in prison.

After a long while, Corrie was released from prison.
She then had no father.
She had no sister. She had no home.

TALK ABOUT IT IN CLASS: If you were Corrie, how would you feel? Would you **love** or
hate those who had killed your family?

Do you know what Corrie did? She chose to **love** those who had killed her father and sister.
She chose to **love** those who had taken away her home. It was not easy to **love** those who
had injured her. But she was a Christian. God commanded her to **love** even her enemies.

TURN IN YOUR BIBLE to **MATTHEW 5:44**.

Fill in the blanks:

Jesus said, "BUT I TELL YOU, _____ YOUR ENEMIES, AND
_____ FOR THOSE WHO PERSECUTE YOU..."

Questions 120 and 121

> <u>**What is the sixth petition?**</u>
> "And lead us not into temptation but deliver us from evil."
>
> <u>**What do we pray for in the sixth petition?**</u>
> That God would keep us from sin.

Shadrach, **Meshach**, and **Abednego** were in trouble!
King Nebuchadnezzar told them to bow down to a false idol, but they would **not**!
Shadrach, **Meshach**, AND **Abednego** were willing to say, "**No!**" when they were told to disobey God! Then they were thrown into the **fiery furnace**!

I WANT YOU TO LEARN **THREE WORDS** TODAY.
These words are TRIAL, TEST, and TEMPTATION!

A **trial** is a **difficulty** in our life that we can choose to use for GOD or for the devil.

When we use the **trial** (like the fiery furnace!) **for God**, then the **trial** becomes a **test**.
When we pass **God's test**, we please Him.

When we use the **trial** (like the fiery furnace, again!) for the devil,
then the **trial** becomes a **temptation**.
When we fall to the **devil's temptation**, we please the devil. We do not please God.

Did the **trial** of the **fiery furnace** become a **test** or a **temptation** to **Shadrach**, **Meshach**, and **Abednego**? _____

Catechism for Young Children

Questions 122 and 123

<u>**How many sacraments are there?**</u> Two. **What are they?** **Baptism and The Lord's Supper.**

Have you ever noticed your church's sanctuary?
Have you noticed that there are certain pieces of furniture in the front of your sanctuary?
There are **three** pieces of furniture in your Church which we want to talk about today.
There is the **pulpit**. There is the **communion table**. There is the **baptismal font**.
Every Church sanctuary should always have these three things.

Now I want you to draw your sanctuary. Pretend that you are a **little bird**.
You are nesting in a place high above your sanctuary.
When you look down on your sanctuary what do you see?

Draw in where the CONGREGATION sits. Draw where the CHOIR sits, or the Worship
Team stands. Of MOST IMPORTANTANCE, draw in the PULPIT, the COMMUNION
TABLE, the BAPTISM FONT, or in some cases, the BAPTISIMAL POOL!

Did you remember where everything is? Your class might want to go into your sanctuary and
see if each student drew things where they ought to be!

Catechism for Young Children

Questions 124 and 125

<u>Who appointed these sacraments?</u>
The Lord Jesus Christ.

<u>Why did Christ appoint these sacraments?</u>
To distinguish His disciples from the world, and to comfort and strengthen them.

In our last lesson, you drew a picture of your sanctuary.
You drew where the **congregation** sits, where the **choir** or **Worship team** sits.
But the most important furniture is not the **pews** or the **choir seats**.
What are the **most important** pieces of furniture in the sanctuary?

1. _____

2. _____

3. _____

The **pulpit** is important because here **God's Word** is **read**.
At the **pulpit**, the **Word of God** is also **preached**. The **pulpit** is very, very important.

Why are the **communion table** and **baptismal font** or the **baptismal pool** important?

The **communion table** is important because _____

_____

The **baptism font** or **pool** is important because _____

_____

The Lord Jesus **appointed** two sacraments. They are **baptism** and the **Lord's Supper**.

To **appoint** means **to choose**, or **to set aside for a purpose**. The Lord Jesus set aside baptism and the **Lord's Supper** for two purposes. Write these two purposes in the blanks.

1. _____

_____

2. _____

_____

Questions 126 and 127 and 128

> **What sign is used in baptism?**
> The washing with water.
>
> **What does this signify?**
> That we are cleansed from sin by the blood of Christ.
>
> **In whose name are we baptized?**
> In the Name of the Father, and of the Son,
> and of the Holy Ghost.

It is very important to realize that **baptism** does not save you. To understand this, we need to review some questions we have learned.

55.   WHO WILL BE SAVED?
56.   WHAT IS IT TO REPENT?
57.   WHAT IS IT TO BELIEVE OR HAVE FAITH IN CHRIST?

Baptism does not save a person. Baptism is a sign. A sign is a **symbol**.

We see **signs** or **symbols** every day. Can you tell what these **road signs** mean?

_____   _____   _____   _____

Baptism is a **sign** or **symbol**. It stands for something that has happened to a person.

Baptism means that we are c_____ from s_____ by the b_____
of C_____.

TURN IN YOUR BIBLE to **MATTHEW 28:18-20**. Fill in this portion of those verses:

"THEREFORE GO AND MAKE DISCIPLES OF ALL NATIONS,

B_____ THEM IN THE NAME OF THE F_____,

AND OF THE S_____, AND OF THE H_____ S_____."

Questions 129 and 130 and 131

Who are to be baptized?
Believers and their children.

Why should infants be baptized?
Because they have a sinful nature and need a Savior.

Does Christ care for little children?
Yes, for He says, "Suffer the little children to come unto me,
and forbid them not: for of such is the kingdom of God."

Have you ever seen a baby baptized?
The parents bring the child to the front of the congregation.
The pastor reads the Bible and then prays. Then the pastor takes a little water,
puts the water on the baby's head, and says,

"Little One (or whatever the baby's name is!), I baptize you
in the Name of the Father, and of the Son, and of the Holy Spirit."

Do you know why babies are baptized?
Write in the answer to Question #130.

1. _____

2. _____

TURN IN YOUR BIBLE TO **ACTS 2:39**.
Peter is speaking. Fill in the missing words of this verse.

ACTS 2:39 "THE PROMISE IS FOR _____ AND FOR YOUR _____ AND FOR ALL WHO ARE FAR OFF...FOR ALL WHOM THE LORD OUR GOD WILL CALL."
We are a part of God's **covenant family**.
God has given to believers great and wonderful promises of salvation.
These same promises are also for the children of believers. We are a part of God's **covenant family**!

I'm so glad
I'm a part of the
Family of God!

Question 132

> **To what does your baptism bind you?**
> To be a true follower of Christ.

When we trust in Christ alone for salvation, we are to walk in His Word and obey Him day by day.

When a child is baptized, the pastor asks the parents three questions.
They are very serious questions because baptism is a very serious commitment.
The parents claim **God's covenant promises** for this little child.
The parents **promise to obey God's word** for this child. The questions:

1. **Do you acknowledge your child's need of the cleansing blood of Jesus Christ, and the renewing grace of the Holy Spirit?**

All of us are sinners. Even babies are born as sinners. Christian parents agree with God that their child is a sinner. Remember these Catechism questions?
35. What effect had the sin of Adam on all mankind?
36. What is that sinful nature called which we inherit from Adam?
37. What does every sin deserve?
38. Can anyone go to Heaven with this sinful nature?
39. What is a change of heart called?
40. Who can change a sinner's heart?

2. **Do you claim God's covenant promises in his/her behalf, and do you look in faith to the Lord Jesus Christ for his/her salvation as you do for your own?**

Christian parents agree to act as Channels of God's Love for their children.

3. **Do you now, unreservedly, dedicate your child to God, and promise, in humble reliance upon divine grace,**
   _____ **that you will endeavor to set a Godly example,**
   _____ **that you will pray with and for him/her,**
   _____ **that you will teach him/her the doctrines of our holy religion,**
   _____ **that you will strive, by all the means of God's appointment, to bring him/her up in the nurture and admonition of the Lord?**

CAN YOU NUMBER THE **FOUR RESPONSIBILITIES** OF THE PARENT FROM THE THIRD QUESTION?
PUT THE NUMBER IN THE BLANK BESIDE THE RESPONSIBILITY: 1,2,3.4.

Catechism for Young Children

Questions 133 and 134 and 135

<u>What is the Lord's Supper?</u>
The eating of bread and drinking of wine
in remembrance of the sufferings and death of Christ.

<u>What does the bread represent?</u>
The body of Christ, broken for our sins.

<u>What does the wine represent?</u>
The blood of Christ, shed for our salvation.

How often does your Church celebrate the
Lord's Supper?

Some Churches celebrate it every three
months. Some Churches celebrate it once
a month.
Some Churches celebrate it every week.
Whatever the time, it is important that all
believers celebrate it.

TURN IN YOUR BIBLE to **MARK 14:12-26**: "The night before Jesus went to the cross,
He gave us The Lord's Supper."

VERSE 14, The Jewish holiday being celebrated _____

VERSE 22, Jesus took the _____, gave thanks and broke it..."

VERSE 23, Jesus took the _____, gave thanks and offered it..."

VERSE 26, What did the Disciples and Jesus do before they went out to the Mount of
Olives? _____

VERSE 22, What does the bread represent? _____

VERSE 24. What does the cup represent? _____

VERSE 25, When will Jesus celebrate the Lord's Supper with us again?_____

_____

Question 136

> ### <u>Who should partake of The Lord's Supper?</u>
> Only those who repent of their sins, believe in Christ for salvation,
> and love their fellow men.

Only **saved** people should come to the Lord's Supper. What does a saved person do?

Question # 55, "WHO WILL BE SAVED?"

The answer to Question 55 is almost like the answer to Question 136.

There are three things that make us ready to come to The Lord's Supper. What are they?

1. _____

2. _____

3. _____

REPENTANCE

Question #56. WHAT IS IT TO REPENT?

   Student, the hardest six words to ever say are, "I was wrong; I am sorry."

   Have you ever had to apologize? It's not fun, is it? But that's what repentance is.

   When we come to The Lord's Supper, we are to repent.

BELIEVE

Question #57. WHAT IS IT TO BELIEVE OR HAVE FAITH IN CHRIST?

   When we come to The Lord's Supper, we may trust that He will accept us.
   We may believe, with certainty, that the Lord Jesus died for us.

LOVE

Question #76. WHAT IS THE SUM OF THE TEN COMMANDMENTS?

   Turn back to the lesson on Question #76. Read that passage from **I JOHN** once again.

Questions 137 and 138 and 139

<u>Did Christ remain in the tomb after his crucifixion?</u>
No, he rose from the tomb on the third day after his death.

<u>Where is Christ now?</u>
In heaven, interceding for sinners.

<u>Will he come again?</u>
Yes, at the last day Christ will come to judge the world.

BEFORE WE GO ON, WE NEED TO REVIEW…. again!
THERE ARE OTHER CATECHISM QUESTIONS WHICH WILL HELP US TO UNDERSTAND TODAY'S LESSON! LOOK
THEM UP AND READ THE ANSWERS.

64. WHAT OFFICES HAS CHRIST?
65. WHAT ARE THEY?
67. HOW IS CHRIST A PRIEST?

88. WHAT DAY OF THE WEEK IS THE CHRISTIAN SABBATH?
89. WHY IS IT CALLED THE LORD'S DAY?

We are sinners. The Lord Jesus came to die for sinners. Three days after He died for us, He rose from the dead. He came out of the tomb. Over 500 people saw Him alive.

After His resurrection, the Lord Jesus went back to Heaven.

For the last 2,000 years, the Lord Jesus has been in Heaven. He has been doing a very special work for us. He has been INTERCEDING for us.

LOOK THIS WORD UP IN A DICTIONARY.

INTERCEDE

The Lord Jesus is INTERCEDING for us who belong to Him.
He is asking His Father that we would come to love Him.
He is asking His Father that we would be kept from evil.
He is asking His Father that we would love one another.
He is asking His Father that we would share the Gospel with others.

Catechism for Young Children

Questions 140 and 141

> **What becomes of men at death?**
> The body returns to dust,
> and the soul goes into the world of spirits.
>
> **Will the bodies of the dead be raised to life again?**
> Yes, "the trumpet shall sound, and the dead shall be raised."

Wow! What a day it's going to be!
The Bible says that one day, everyone all over the world will hear a trumpet blast.
It will be a trumpet blast for Heaven!

And right as the trumpet is blowing, graves will rip open!
From these graves, believers will fly forth! They will be flying up to meet the Lord Jesus!

And at that same time, believers who are still alive on earth will begin to fly upward too.
They also will fly forth to meet the Lord Jesus!

What a day it's going to be! You can read about it in the Bible.

TURN IN YOUR BIBLE TO
I THESSALONIANS 4:16 and 17.

Fill in these blanks from
I THESSALONIANS 4:16 and 17:

"FOR THE _____

HIMSELF WILL COME DOWN FROM HEAVEN,

WITH A LOUD_____,

WITH THE VOICE OF THE _____,

AND WITH THE_____.

CALL OF GOD AND THE DEAD IN CHRIST WILL RISE FIRST. AFTER THAT, WE WHO ARE STILL ALIVE AND ARE LEFT WILL BE CAUGHT UP WITH THEM IN THE CLOUDS TO MEET THE LORD IN THE AIR."

Questions 142 and 143

What will become of the wicked in the day of judgment?
They shall be cast into hell.

What is hell?
A place of dreadful and endless torment.

Dear, dear Student,
Hell is such a horrible, an awful place.
I just don't want to spend much time talking about it.

But we need to know **5** things about hell.

1. Hell is very **real**.
    It is not a make-pretend story.

2. People go to hell.
    People go to hell because they reject the Lord Jesus. They turn their backs on Him.

3. People do not have to go to hell.
    They can go to **heaven** instead. God has made the way by sending Jesus for us. We may reach to Him, He is there. We may take His hand. He offers it to help and to save us.

4. There is only **one way not** to go to hell.
    The way not to go to hell is to trust in the Lord Jesus.

5. God commands us to tell others about the Lord Jesus.
    We are to tell others about the Lord Jesus so that they will trust in Him and go to **heaven**.

Questions 144 and 145

> **What will become of the righteous?**
> They shall be taken to Heaven.
>
> **What is heaven?**
> A glorious and happy place where the righteous shall be forever with the Lord.

I don't like to think about hell, but I **love** to think about **heaven**!

What do you think **heaven** is going to be like?
The Bible tells us some things about **heaven**, but it does not tell us **everything** about **heaven**!

Boy, are we going to be surprised when we get there!
Heaven is going to be so much better than we ever imagined!
It's going to be **bigger**!
It's going to be **brighter**!
It's going to be **better** than our best dreams here!

We can **think** about heaven. We can **dream** about heaven. We can **talk** about heaven.

We must read the Bible to find out about heaven. The Bible is like a telescope, showing us a little of heaven.

TURN IN YOUR BIBLE to **REVELATION 21:1-4**.
WRITE DOWN 3 things that you can know about heaven.

1. _____

2. _____

3. _____

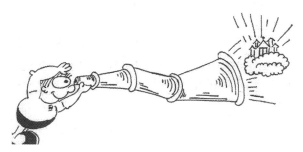

By the way, Kitty and I are going to heaven. Will we see **you** there? We very much want to!

What the Others Say about the WB: (Quotes)

1. As a classroom teacher in 1985, I was hired to teach Catechism classes for 1st, 3rd, 5th graders, and to write a Bible curriculum for a private Christian school. Even with certification for elementary education and special education, I could not have accomplished this without the "rough draft," of this work by my good friend, Tom Weaver. It saved my job! With it, I was able to prepare for and teach these classes. Since that time, my three children and others have memorized these questions and answers, recited them at one sitting, and have benefited personally from the definitions and concepts.

   — Nancy Morgan,
   BS Winthrop University, Elementary and Special Education

2. My children were in this Catechism class and others in our church and home school. I now teach Latin in our K-12 Classical School. I want this Catechism Workbook on my shelf of resources. I want it in hand for my future grandchildren. Tom Weaver has been our friend!

   — Melodi Sigler
   University of Texas, BS in Speech, Language Pathology
   University of Houston, Masters, Speech, Language Pathology

3. When I was shown this Workbook, I asked to review it and quickly said it needed to be published. At 94, I have known the presence of God since I was 12 years old. While reviewing these lessons, every time I turned a page, I learned something new! Seeing its value for children and families, I immediately encouraged Emily toward the publishing process.

   — Dottie Hogue
   University Mississippi, BA Journalism
   Columnist, Yazoo Herald

4. So super glad that you are publishing this great workbook! Hilarious and poignant stories beautifully illustrate each lesson's question and answer! We have really enjoyed the glimpse into these life stories, helping us to personally apply the lessons. The girls love the cute pictures and enjoy responding with color and their own art. This Workbook is of value to our Home-school curriculum!

   — Leigh Graf
   Bob Jones University
   BA, MA Interpretive Speech, Performing Arts

5. It has been an honor to serve alongside Emily Weaver for Vespers, a ministry meeting the spiritual needs of the aging and people with dementia. It did not surprise me when Emily shared with us her heart-felt desire to publish the Catechism Workbook, written and illustrated by her husband, Tom and then taught by them both. We are blessed to support this project which will leave a legacy of Tom and Emily's ministry here on earth.

   — Monte Estes
   Monte Estes Texas A&M University, College Station, Civil Engineering
   Andi Estes, Loan Officer, Associate Manager, Caregiver

6. As a former third grade teacher, I would have loved to use this Bible curriculum in my private school classroom. I have personally taught this study in my home, and it is excellent. Our world needs more curriculum like this in the hands of families so that parents can easily teach these *essential truths* in our age of humanism and questionable culture. I look forward to seeing how God uses this project to impact the lives of elementary students and strengthen their faith in Jesus!

   — Elizabeth Hewitt
   A&M University, Corpus Christi
   BA Elementary Education, multiple certifications

7. If we want the next generation to stand firm against the moral chaos of our modern world, we must give them a firm foundation. This workbook is an excellent resource for teaching children the essential doctrines of the Christian faith in a way that is simple to understand, yet uncompromising on biblical truth.

   — Reed Hewitt, Communications Professional
   A&M University, Corpus Christi, Texas
   LivingStrategically.com

8. Tom and Emily Weaver created a phenomenal work that expounds God's truths in a way children can easily comprehend. The stories and illustrations in the workbook simply and succinctly explain these truths, providing a strong Biblical foundation for future growth. The workbook has been a blessing to our family.

   — Randy Wipke
   Texas A&M U, College Station, Building Construction
   — Carol Wipke
   Prairie View A&M University, Elementary Education

9. You hold in your hands a valuable tool for training up the next generation in the eternal truths of God's Word! When my husband and I began teaching at African Bible University near Kampala, Uganda in 2008, our African students said, "Come and teach us rightly so that we may go and teach others rightly!" They will use this engaging workbook by Tom and Emily Weaver to train children and adults "rightly," providing them with a firm foundation during shaky times. I am eager to place it in their hands!

    — Cheri Hoke, Instructor, African Bible University, Uganda
    Texas Tech University, BS, Elementary Education
    University of Missouri, Kan City, MS, Learning Disabilities

10. It is a challenge to find materials that teach children foundational truths and moral values including who they are and why they are here. This workbook is based on a proven and successful method of instruction. Complex truths within the Word of God are simplified but not compromised. This book will serve as a wonderful resource for parents, teachers, and grandparents. It will help give their children information that will ground and steady them throughout their entire lives.

    — Roberta Nelson
    Bob Jones University, BS, Elementary Education
    Texas A&M, Corpus Christi, MS Counseling

Printed in the United States
by Baker & Taylor Publisher Services